THE JESUS
PRIORITIES

THE JESUS PRIORITIES

ESSENTIAL HABITS

8

CHRISTOPHER MARICLE

UPPER ROOM BOOKS®
NASHVILLE

THE JESUS PRIORITIES
8 Essential Habits

Copyright © 2007 by Christopher Maricle
All rights reserved.

Cover and interior design: Gore Studio, Inc. / gorestudio.com
First printing: 2007

LIBRARY OF CONGRESS CATALOGING-IN-PUBLICATION DATA

Maricle, Christopher, 1963–
  Jesus priorities : eight essential habits / Christopher Maricle.
     p. cm.
  Includes bibliographical references and index.
  ISBN 978-0-8358-9914-7 (alk. paper)
  1. Christian life. I. Title.
  BV4501.3.M258 2007
  248.4—dc22   2007021071

Printed in the United States of America

For my wife, Anne.
Her deep faith in God has always been a source of grace for me.
Her belief in me and in this dream has been a great blessing.

For my children, Sarah and Nicholas.
No one has taught me more about patience, forgiveness, and love.

For our parents,
Herb and Jan and Frank and Joan,
for all the love and support.

For my brothers and sisters,
Cathy, Steve, Brian, Susie, and Julie.
We don't say it nearly enough, so I wrote it here: I love you.

Special thanks to my parents for the Bible
they gave me for Christmas in 1988. It was in this
now well-worn Bible that I read and studied the Gospels.
The inscription reads simply: "To Chris with love from
Mom and Dad. Pray for us." The word of God
could not be more precious to me.

CONTENTS

Contents

ACKNOWLEDGMENTS

Great thanks to my wife, Anne, my father, Herb, and my brother Brian. Their patience with me and their insightful reading and editing were terrific.

I am sincerely grateful to Sister Marian Clare Valenteen, a great boss and a terrific friend; our coffee chats about God, faith, prayer, and life have been so helpful to me. The encouragement from so many people kept me going, including brother Steve, Anne Duffy, Frank Hamill, Sister Gloria de Jesus, and Sister Terry Davis.

Thanks to Bill Davis for his assistance. A special thanks to Laurie Beth Jones for thinking this project intriguing enough to pursue and to Terry Barber for his encouragement and advice.

Thank you to Upper Room Books, especially Denise Duke for helping me keep my facts straight, Jeannie Crawford-Lee for assistance in editing, and Lynne Deming for believing in this idea.

Warm thanks and a high five to my children, Sarah and Nick, for their additions to the text.

PREFACE

How Did I Start this Journey?

In April of 2000 my son was born with serious medical complications. He had no spleen; some of his internal organs were in the wrong place; and he had a small hole in his heart. His chances of surviving past the age of five were less than 5 percent. Two years later, my wife bravely endured a life-threatening illness. The aggressive treatment lasted nearly a year, as did her recovery from treatment. I have prayed the desperate and pleading prayer of Gethsemane many times and found no answers.

I needed answers to these questions that are so fundamental to Christian living. Why is this life, at times, so hard? Why isn't my faith helping me? Why am I finding no comfort in prayer? These questions—and the struggles behind them—challenged all my notions of faith, my perception of God, and the purpose of this life.

At first I could not understand why I did not already know the answers I needed. I was raised Catholic. I went to Catholic elementary and high school. I attended Catholic colleges for some undergraduate and most of my postgraduate training. I taught in Catholic schools for five years and have served as a Catholic school administrator for fifteen years. For decades I thought I had the "God thing" all figured out. After more than thirty years of being Catholic, imagine my surprise at learning that I needed to get to know my God a lot better.

THE JESUS PRIORITIES

How They Add Up

Aɴᴛʜᴏɴʏ ᴅᴇ Mᴇʟʟᴏ, a Jesuit priest and teacher, once said, "This is what is ultimate in our human knowledge of God, to know that we do not know."[1] Indeed, God knows that we cannot understand the divine, and that is why God sent Jesus. Jesus Christ came to reveal to imperfect humans with limited understanding the nature of our perfect God. "If you knew me, you would know my Father" (John 8:19). Jesus told us that we could find God through him; so developing an intimate understanding of Jesus through his life and teachings is central to that goal. This deep hope and desire to find God through Jesus drove me to the Gospels, to refocus my life on the message of Jesus.

The Gospels are the best windows to the truth for Christians; they are an invaluable source of faith to us. While it is true that humans wrote the Gospels and that they therefore reflect our human imperfection, their formation was also God-inspired; so the Gospels contain God's holy guidance. This book is predicated upon an unfailing trust in this divine guidance. Everything the evangelists wrote may not be completely accurate, but it seems reasonable to believe that the Gospels were written because God wanted them written. Further, it seems reasonable to trust that God's inspiration and grace ensured that the most important ideas for us were mentioned numerous times so that we would be sure to notice them. This belief led me to develop two assumptions as guides for my study.

Assumption 1: God earnestly desires us to find God. God is love, and love seeks unity. As a gift, Jesus came to help us find the way to

God, to lead the way. He encouraged us to follow him, so it must be within our power to do so. He would not have left us instructions we could not follow, for "is there anyone among you who, if your child asks for bread, will give a stone?" (Matt. 7:9, NRSV).

Assumption 2: Because Jesus wants us to find our way to God, he left directions, or instructions, that could be found easily. He left them in the memory of his life, in his teachings and actions recorded in the Gospels. The Gospels are not just for bishops, priests, theologians, or scholars. The Good News was preached to all: "Let anyone with ears to hear listen!" (Mark 4:9, NRSV). The Gospels, inspired by God and written by human hands, are a gift to each of us. We needn't be learned theologians—or even read their work—to explore the messages contained in the Gospels. Through study, reflection, and prayer anybody can find Jesus' message.

When we want our children to find Easter eggs on Easter Sunday morning, we know how to ensure the eggs are found. We make a lot of them, we color them brightly, and we place them where others can see them. Jesus did the same thing. He left his ministry, the example of his life, the stories of his teachings and actions recorded for us in the Gospels, and he called attention to the most important things by saying or doing them many times.

It was with these assumptions that I began my study of the words and actions of Jesus to answer a single question:

What did Jesus consistently say and do during his public ministry that would be instructive for us?

To answer this question, I organized the events of Jesus' story to reveal recurring ideas. These themes emerged by categorizing Jesus' words and actions by general concepts and then cross-referencing the four Gospels to determine how many times a particular idea or event occurred and how many times it was recorded in the Gospels. By focusing on these themes, the priorities emerged not from any single Gospel passage but from a synthesis of Jesus' actions and teachings.

What did Jesus...

Our focus here is on what Jesus said and did. Consideration of the words and actions of the apostles or church doctrine is not part of this book's scope. The focus is on Jesus.

consistently say and do ...

Isolated incidents reveal little about an individual, but reflecting on patterns of behavior reveals the content of a person's character and the values that person holds. The way we spend our time and resources is an expression of our values. Jesus told us this himself when he taught us that "each tree is known by its own fruit" (Luke 6:44). So reflecting on how Jesus spent his time should be instructive. What did he say over and over again? What did he do repeatedly? The key word here is *consistently*.

during his public ministry ...

We will be looking at what Jesus said and did during his public ministry. I highlight only those events that were open to all, in which anyone was free to follow him, to hear his teachings, observe his healings, and to witness his miracles. His public ministry was accessible to everyone. It makes sense to ask the question: *When Jesus had the greatest potential for touching as many hearts as possible, what was he doing?* For the purposes of this investigation, I have defined the public ministry of Jesus as beginning with his baptism by John the Baptist (Matt. 3:14-17; Mark 1:9-11) and ending with the commencement of the Last Supper (Matt. 26:20; Mark 14:17; Luke 22:14; John 13).

that would be instructive for us?

By *instructive* I mean the behavior of Jesus that we can adopt: the essential habits we can incorporate in our daily life. From an analysis of those things Jesus consistently said and did, I have tried to distill the actions of Jesus that are accessible to us—those we can learn and apply practically.

Would Jesus Approve?

This approach to Gospel study seems consistent with Jesus' own use of scripture. Jesus was concerned with the spirit of the law, not the letter of the law. He used metaphors and similes on a regular basis; he employed colorful and illustrative language to develop themes in terms and contexts his listeners could absorb. Therefore seeking to synthesize the words and actions of Jesus into themes is consistent with the example of Christ.

The Jesus Priorities is the result of that effort. I hope it will inspire you to return to the Gospels, to reflect more deeply on the life of Christ, and to divine from Jesus how to best live your life in a way that is faithful to the mission Jesus entrusted to his disciples and, through them, to us.

What Are the Eight Priorities?

Why organize the words and actions of Jesus to reveal themes? Remember that the Gospels were first passed on in an oral tradition. Since the story of Jesus was initially preserved through storytelling, it makes sense that the stories were generally organized from beginning to end. Using time as the organizing principle made the story easy to recall and to share. The written Gospels continued this tradition by organizing the story of Jesus chronologically.

Most church-attending Christians have heard the gospel story many times. Proclaimed to the assembly at Sunday services following the church calendar and liturgical seasons, the stories have been told from beginning to end. Our spiritual needs do not necessarily follow this pattern of time and seasons though. Despite half a lifetime of familiarity with the gospel story, my understanding of the gospel message was not sufficient when crisis struck. My need to go deeper into Christ's story compelled me to look at Christ's life in new ways. It occurred to me that applying a different organizing principle might reveal different ideas or at least new insights into the teachings Jesus gave us in his life and preaching. As I read and literally started counting the number of times Jesus mentioned certain ideas, patterns began to emerge. These patterns provide the organizing principle for this book: Jesus' most repeated words and actions reveal eight priorities.

In these pages you will find an alternative approach to reading the Gospels. Rather than read them chronologically, you can draw from several gospel stories and reflect on how our struggles are illuminated by what Jesus said and did about those same challenges. Certainly the message of Christ cannot be reduced to numbers, but the numbers can be revealing. They provide a metric, however crude, for measuring how much time and energy Jesus put into some of his teachings. The results are summarized in table 1 on the next page.

Classifying the Priorities

For each priority, I have established the total number of events, that is, the number of times Jesus said or did something, as well as calculated the total number of times that event was recorded in the four Gospels. One challenging factor is the reality that some events could be placed under two or more themes. I have placed the parable of the prodigal son, for example, in *Love*. It could also be justifiably classified under *Heal* or even *Humility*. However, to avoid confusion, most events have not been assigned to more than one category.

Exploring the Priorities

We will explore each of these eight priorities and the essential habit each one calls us to develop. First, though, some general findings deserve mention. The eight priorities can be divided, like the Ten Commandments, into two primary categories. *Pray* and *Seek God's Will* provide guidance for building our relationship with God. These priorities reveal the fundamental habits of thought and the elements of personal faith essential for life in God. *Heal, Love, Spread the Word, Build Up Treasure in Heaven, Accept Children as Precious,* and *Live with Humility* describe our relationship with people. They provide guidance on essential habits for Christian life as it is lived in action, giving clear direction on how to treat all people, all neighbors.

ADDING UP THE JESUS PRIORITIES

Priority	Events	Recordings
Heal	36	63
Love	24	35
Pray	23	32
Spread the Word	18	36
Treasure in Heaven	12	25
Seek God's Will	14	16
Children as Precious	6	14
Live with Humility	9	12

Table 1

Some simple addition reveals that the set of priorities about God includes 37 events recorded 48 times. In comparison, the number of events and recordings for the second set of priorities—about how to treat others—are 105 and 185 respectively. Jesus spent a lot more time teaching us how to treat each other. For Jesus, how we treat others is at least important as how we treat God.

The Top Three Priorities

What did Jesus consistently say and do during his public ministry that would be instructive for us? A substantial portion of the answer lies in the top three priorities. More than anything else, Jesus consistently acted out the importance of healing, love, and prayer. It is also instructive to see that two of the top three priorities focus on how we should treat other people. Of the three, only prayer is directly concerned with our relationship with God. By considering either the number of events or the number of recordings, the first three priorities are standouts. In fact, the events and recording for the first three priorities account for almost 60 percent of the total for all eight priorities.[2]

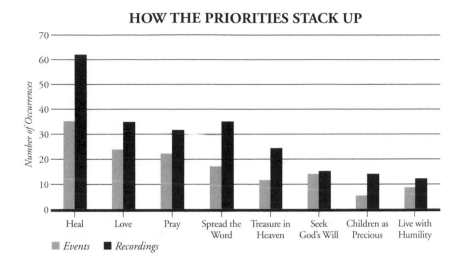

HOW THE PRIORITIES STACK UP

Number of Occurrences

Heal | Love | Pray | Spread the Word | Treasure in Heaven | Seek God's Will | Children as Precious | Live with Humility

■ *Events* ■ *Recordings*

How To Read and Use *The Jesus Priorities*

With the Bible

This book does not stand on its own. It is a guide to the gospel of Jesus. As you work through *The Jesus Priorities*, use your Bible actively, looking up events and checking cross-references. It was not practical to refer in the text to every event that contributed to determining the priorities, but I encourage you to read and reflect on all the Gospel accounts related to each priority. The Appendix provides a complete listing of each Gospel event and where it occurs in each of the four Gospel narratives.

With Others

This book is not meant to be read in isolation. It certainly can serve as a vehicle for private spiritual reflection, but I hope it will also start conversations. Share your discoveries, insights, and disagreements with others, and sustain a dialogue about how all of us can best live a life pleasing to God and Christ.

With Action

This book is not meant to be read and then set aside. Merely reading it will not yield spiritual growth. As you study the priorities, think about how to translate them into essential habits for your life. The specific circumstances of your life change, sometimes from year to year, sometimes from day to day. Amid this change are two constants: (1) the fundamental challenges of life and (2) Jesus' priorities.

By continuously reflecting on what Jesus said and did, you will be able to stay focused on the path that Christ showed us during his public ministry. Working with *The Jesus Priorities* should lead to changes in behavior as you commit to new habits by integrating the priorities of Jesus into your daily living.

With Discipline

Acting differently is possible only when we think differently, because all our actions flow from our thoughts. Before we can act like Jesus, we have to think like Jesus. Reflecting on and studying Jesus' priorities challenges us first to change our way of thinking. The priorities call us to see the world as Jesus sees it. When we begin to perceive our world as Jesus does, we will be motivated—even compelled—to act like Jesus, to cultivate the habits he modeled.

At the end of each chapter, a section titled "From Jesus Priority to Essential Habit" outlines four steps to help you begin thinking—and acting—differently.

1. Review a summary of Jesus' practices that demonstrate the essential habit.
2. Reflect on a Gospel passage expressing Jesus' priority.
3. Reflect on your own priorities with suggested questions.
4. Pray for God's help in living the Jesus priorities.

It takes discipline to stay gospel-focused. Some years ago, when I was working with a school faculty on how to respond to inappropriate student behavior, I looked up *discipline* in the dictionary. I was surprised by what I found: "Discipline is instruction having for its aim to form the pupil to proper conduct and action" and "mental or moral training." In simple terms, *discipline* is a mental endeavor.

You will note that *discipline* is rooted in the word *disciple*. Jesus put his disciples on the path of training, and they certainly did not "get it" right away. Indeed, long after Jesus had completed his public ministry, his disciples were still asking questions. After three years with Jesus, they knew more than when they started, but they still needed training. As imperfect humans, reading the Gospels once through and then applying them as best we can is not enough. Real devotion to the teachings of Jesus requires constant attention, action, and reflection. That takes discipline.

Like the first apostles, we too need a program of training. Weekly church services that follow a chronological cycle of Gospel story reflections set the stage for spiritual growth; attending such services is an important part of our involvement with our faith community. Jesus and his friends went to the synagogue too, but they did so much more! We need to do more as well. We need to do what Jesus did with his apostles: act out and reflect upon God's love on a daily basis.

The Jesus Priorities provides a resource to do just that. By continuously reflecting on Jesus' priorities, we can bring all that Jesus said and did to bear on the questions and struggles of daily living. We will train ourselves to think differently about our world, and we will begin to act differently—to develop the habits that flow from the Jesus priorities. We will devote ourselves more to healing, loving, praying, spreading the word, building up treasure in heaven, seeking God's will, accepting children, and living with humility.

JESUS PRIORITY 1

Heal

GOSPEL STORY— *The Syrophoenician Woman*

And behold, a Canaanite woman from that region came out and cried, "Have mercy on me, O Lord, Son of David; my daughter is severely possessed by a demon." But he did not answer her a word. And his disciples came and begged him, saying, "Send her away, for she is crying after us." He answered, "I was sent only to the lost sheep of the house of Israel." But she came and knelt before him, saying, "Lord, help me." And he answered, "It is not fair to take the children's bread and throw it to the dogs." She said, "Yes, Lord, yet even the dogs eat the crumbs that fall from their masters' table." Then Jesus answered her, "O woman, great is your faith! Be it done for you as you desire." And her daughter was healed instantly.

—MATTHEW 15:22-28

JESUS HEALED PEOPLE more than any other action he takes in the Gospels.[1] If we learn nothing else from his public ministry, we should learn this: Jesus consistently healed others. In doing so, he left us four principles we can adopt: compassion, saying yes to strangers, doing what is in our power to do, and seeing with the heart.

HEAL THROUGH COMPASSION

Jesus' concern for healing is well documented. There are at least fifteen events recorded twenty times in which Jesus heals others while doing something else. We find no details; usually a single sentence or even just a phrase notes the episodes. These miracles are mentioned almost in passing, as if Jesus' ability to heal had become commonplace. In Matthew 8:16 (compare Mark 1:32-34 and Luke 4:40-41) we read, "they brought to him many who were possessed with demons; and he cast out the spirits with a word, and healed all who were sick." In Mark 6:5: "he laid his hands on a few sick people and healed them." In Luke 9:11: "he welcomed them and spoke to them of the kingdom of God, and cured those who had need of healing."

The frequency with which Jesus healed is simply astonishing; his constant attention to the suffering of others sets a standard that few in history have come close to attaining. Although healing people was not Jesus' primary mission, compassion was central to his daily life because it demonstrated God's love so profoundly—the message proclaimed by Jesus.

Compassion not only benefits others but also frees us. When we adopt a compassionate spirit, we let go of hostility, prejudice, and even fear. Carrying these emotions around demands a lot of our time and energy. Jesus never gave these negative attitudes any energy; he focused all his energy on compassion. Jesus' habit of compassion lies at the heart of all his acts of healing, and this motivation is all the more evident in these Gospel "sidebars," where he appears to act spontaneously, while traveling or otherwise engaged. No matter what he was doing, Jesus never let go of this compassion.

Just as the things Jesus consistently said and did reveal the content of his character and the fundamental values he held, so do our daily words and actions define us. At some point in the past our daily habits may have represented choices, but since then they have devolved into routine. We begin to do them or say them without thinking, without consciously deciding. It has been said that we make our habits, and then our habits make us. Changing habits is hard because they become automatic. Altering them requires us to re-decide, to revisit our values.

The most obvious examples of habits we try to change are diet and exercise. People I know who have successfully lost weight and kept it off made conscious changes in their personal values. They decided that being fit in the long term was more valuable to them than short-term gratification of eating tasty and usually fattening foods. After they redefined their values, they adopted new behaviors to reflect those values. Then they practiced the new behaviors regularly and integrated them into their daily lives until they became habitual.

This is what Jesus did: he integrated activities that flowed directly from his values into his daily routine. Matching words and actions to core beliefs is the very definition of integrity. Jesus had perfect integrity because what he believed was perfectly aligned with what he said and how he acted.

Compassion not only benefits others but also frees us.

To make healing a habit, we may need to examine the unconscious values behind our actions or inactions. The question of these values—or our awareness of them—is not limited to the habit of healing. Truly each of our actions—every choice—represents a value. These actions and their underlying values are chosen over other potential actions with different underlying values. Losing sight of the values that lie beneath our behavior can make us frustrated or bored with our routines.

Probably no one understands this more than stay-at-home parents. Society still fails to properly value adults who leave their profession or postpone entry into the workplace to raise children. The daily chores of washing children's clothes, feeding them, playing with them, disciplining them, and so forth can seem so boring, so redundant.

These routines become less mundane and more connected to God when we are deeply conscious of the values behind these behaviors. Caring for children—teaching them civility, patience, how to stand in line, how to forgive, how to be compassionate—is one of the greatest goals and needs of a civilized society. Few things are more important than fashioning young souls. Staying deeply and consciously connected to this value can help parents. They should resist reinforcing negative attitudes about a particular chore that's distasteful: "I'm dealing with a temper tantrum." Instead, give voice to the overarching value of all the tasks: "I'm forming a young soul by serving as the first model of love."

Jesus maintained this kind of connection to underlying values. Jesus' priority of healing was driven by his constant attention to the value of compassion for the suffering. He acted on this value constantly. We are challenged by Jesus' priority of healing to be deeply conscious of the value of compassion for suffering.

SAY YES TO STRANGERS

The story of the Syrophoenician woman is compelling. This woman, unknown to Jesus, has no claim on him because she is neither family nor close friend. Nor is she a disciple or follower of Jesus. She is not even Jewish. But when she persists in faith and humility, Jesus extends to her the same healing that he gave to Peter's mother-in-law.

Jesus never turned down a request for real need; he responded to each one. It's important to note that a majority of the people Jesus healed were, by our standards, strangers. Even more significant, we must recognize that Jesus had a different standard; he did not make such a distinction at all. In healing others, Jesus treated strangers no differently than he treated his closest friends.

The only real difference between a friend and a stranger is that we are familiar with the former but not the latter. Why do we let this unfamiliarity impede our compassion or generosity? Why do the familiar have a better claim on our time or talent? That we ought not to make this distinction is precisely the message Jesus communicates. "If you love those who love you, what reward do you have? Do not even the tax collectors do the same? And if you greet only your brothers and sisters, what more are you doing than others? Do not even the Gentiles do the same?" (Matt. 5:46-47, NRSV).

Probably no one in recent times has better demonstrated this principle than Mother Teresa. The first mission Mother Teresa founded,

Nirmal Hriday, has treated over one hundred thousand people. She created, by her example, the renowned Missionaries of Charity. The religious order, established in 1950, now has a worldwide presence, serving the most needy in Asia, Africa, Europe, North and Latin America, and Australia. Before the year 2000, an international association of coworkers with more than one million members assisted the order. The order itself continues to grow in numbers every year at a time when most orders are declining. Are not the efforts and achievements of Mother Teresa miraculous?

Mother Teresa was once asked what she believed to be most important in the formation of her novices. She said that the nuns must develop a deep personal love for Jesus and then "go out and find Jesus in their neighbor, and they will serve him in the poor."[2]

This lesson, consistently modeled by Jesus and so beautifully lived out by Mother Teresa, may be the single greatest challenge of the Gospels: treat all humans as you would your dearest family. Our mission, the one we inherit and accept as disciples of Jesus, is to create a world where we extend our capacity for healing to everyone because there are no longer any strangers.

Find a way to say yes. If you cannot give what is asked, give something. Compassion asks you to prepare new scripts for yourself, and to plan for the moment of decision. Take a few minutes to get ready for the next opportunity. What will you say the next time you're asked for help? Be creative; have a kindhearted response ready.

Do What Is within Your Power to Do

Jesus responded with compassion to the human need that confronted him. Even when he was not asked, he brought healing to those suffering around him. He alleviated suffering in a proactive way, a practice illustrated in Luke's story of the widow at Nain in Luke 7:11-17. Upon his arrival at Nain Jesus encounters a funeral procession for a young man, the only son of his widowed mother. Jesus responds to the widow's despair and moves to act. He tells her not to weep and restores her son to life.

In John's Gospel, Jesus heals a man who had been paralyzed for thirty-eight years: "When Jesus saw him and knew that he had been lying there a long time, he said to him, 'Do you want to be healed?'" (John 5:6). Jesus approached him out of compassion for his suffering and with the confidence that he could change it.

In both examples we see how the three behaviors of possessing a dedication to compassion, saying yes to strangers, and doing what is within your power to are modeled perfectly by Jesus. As we strive to emulate this commitment to be a source of healing, we are faced with a question: With a finite ability for impacting the lives of others, how do we imitate Christ in this regard? Once we stay connected to compassion and approach strangers as friends, what action do we take? What is within our power?

A Japanese folk tale gives us some insight about recognizing our power. There once was a stonecutter. While working at the bench in front of his shop, he saw the emperor approaching, carried in a sedan chair by four servants. As the emperor passed, each citizen had to bow down. When the emperor reached the stonecutter, he bowed respectfully. As he did, he thought, *Now, that's power. The emperor is the most powerful man in the world. He can have anything he wants. I wish I could be the emperor.*

And he magically became the emperor. He gave orders, and they were followed. He demanded things, and they were given him. One day he passed through the city in a sedan chair carried by four servants. The sun beat down upon him; the sweat ran down the sides of his face. He looked up and thought, "Now that is power. The sun is the most powerful thing in all the heavens. Nothing can surpass the power of the sun. I wish I could be the sun."

This pattern of wish fulfillment continued. Each time he became what he believed to be the most powerful force, the former stonecutter confronted another power he perceived as superior. As the sun, he is surprised that a storm cloud can block his warming rays. As a storm cloud, he is stunned that his torrential rains can be displaced by the wind. As the wind, he marvels that a stone is immune to his efforts.

Finally he became a stone. He was steadfast and unyielding. He could not be moved because of his great size, and he was unaffected by sun, rain, wind, or even time, for a stone is ageless. He remained so until the day when he felt his very substance being altered, shaped by external forces he could not prevent. He looked up and saw a stonecutter. *He who can fashion the very stones according to his will is mighty indeed. That is power. I wish I could be a stonecutter.*

Like the stonecutter, each of us has power. The challenge is identifying what power we possess and then exercising it in a responsible way. How can we use our power to contribute to the mission that Jesus gave us—extending God's compassion to others? As humans we are limited. Much of life involves learning that many things are simply beyond our power to control.

Beyond Our Power

For many of us, requests for healing are our most urgent prayers. When loved ones suffer, we want them to be healed. Indeed, it is in the midst of suffering that many turn—or return—to God. When medicine and science offer no answers, we look to heaven and hope for the miraculous. I mentioned in the introduction some of my primary reasons for undertaking this study and writing project. I have struggled deeply with the need for healing in my family. In prayer, I have been a beggar before God, pleading for the healing of my wife and my son. But what I wanted really was cure. Healing is more than cure. A cure solves a medical problem. Healing means coming to peace with the way things are. Pondering whether God responds to specific prayer requests for cure or healing raises profound questions. Does suffering serve God's purpose? Does God stretch forth a hand to take an active role in this world? Does God heal if we ask often enough? Do our prayer requests alter the course of events, or is our future predetermined?

Jesus never answered these kinds of questions. When asked about the future and the end times, he said, "Of that day and hour no one knows, not even the angels of heaven, nor the Son, but the Father only"

(Matt. 24:36). The lesson to draw from Jesus' example can't be "miraculously heal others" because we simply don't have that power. We have to be at peace knowing that we cannot control the events that happen every day all around us. They are beyond our power. Jesus did what he could; we must also do what is within our power to do.

Within Our Power

So shall we pray for cure? Jesus, like God, does not cure every person or wipe out all disease. Experience tells us that the cures we pray for—for others or ourselves—are not always granted. However, Jesus did cure people, and he sent his apostles out to "heal the sick, raise the dead, cleanse lepers, cast out demons" (Matt. 10:8). As we shall see in chapter 3, Jesus modeled prayer that focuses on our being an agent of God's will. Praying for healing can be a powerful expression of compassion for others and ourselves. When we offer prayers for cure and healing within the larger framework of our intent to be an agent of God's will, we are responding in the same way that Jesus did—acting out of a deep, heartfelt compassion for others in their suffering. I've often been tempted to think something as ephemeral as prayer or compassion holds minimal value. Neither seems to exert tangible or immediate effect. We can be seduced into believing these acts are of little worth.

Each of us has the power to be a source of healing.

I have a constant reminder that this is not so. A small magnet on our refrigerator says: "We can do no great things, only small things with great love."

Beyond prayer, what can we do? Most humans don't have the power to miraculously cure physical ailments. Consider that Jesus, who was all-powerful, also did not cure all illnesses or disease. He even told us "the poor you always have with you" (John 12:8). As I have struggled with these issues and poured over the Gospels in what I could rightly call a crisis of faith, I have come to accept one fundamental truth. God created the world for love because that is the Almighty's nature. God is love.

Love is creative; God created us to love one another as an expression of his love. God is concerned with our spirit's capacity for love, because love is eternal. The goal of all creation is to join with, or return to, God's love. The task of this life, this physical experience that we spiritual beings share together, is a task of love. It is the choices that flow from our spirit that matter. Life is the stage upon which each of us responds to the life-events that are beyond our power by choosing between love and indifference. Both are within our power.

Each of has the power to be a source of healing because we are each created in God's image and God is love. Love is always within our power to give. What we choose to do with our power is the measure of our willingness to serve God by sharing his love. Healing others requires effort; it is an intentional work. In these gospel stories of healing, Jesus extends himself. He goes out of his way to act on requests that were not part of his immediate plan. He loved those who were suffering by doing what was in his power to do.

Heeding the example of Jesus to do what is in our power to do means that we need to worry less about what happens to us and more about what happens because of us. Being a source of healing means exercising our capacity to love. Love is within our power. In the act of loving unselfishly we touch that part of God's spirit within us. Touching this love is healing both for us and for those to whom we reach out.

SEE WITH THE HEART

Before responding to the need for compassion, we need to recognize it. We can increase our awareness of others' needs by looking with the intent not to judge but to empathize. As an elementary school principal, I have developed a technique for helping young people resolve hurt feelings. It works with first graders and high school students alike. Any adult can use this technique.

I ask the two parties simply to look into each other's eyes. I ask, "How does that person feel?" If they claim not to know, I say, "Look again." I make sure they look each other in the eyes. I have noted that the older the child, the more difficult it is to gaze into the eyes of another for more than a few seconds. Even for young children, it is not easy.

Most children will try first to defend their own actions, even when they've not been asked. Often the first exchange consists of "he said—she said," a natural response because experience tells them someone must take the blame for whatever happened. I intervene by saying, "I know that you are excited, but you are not in trouble. I am not asking who did it. I want to be sure that Joey understands how you feel, and that you understand his feelings. So let's start with you. Don't tell me why; just tell me how Joey feels." Usually the one who isn't crying looks into the eyes of the one who is, then turns and concludes, "He feels sad." From there we explore the reason for the sadness and how it can be avoided in the future. The important part is the act of looking into the eyes of another to answer a question. *How does that person feel? What does that person need?*

We tend not to find those things for which we are not searching, so the questions we ask are critical. They guide our sight. Regarding others without a particular intent limits our vision to the mechanical activity of visually sensing our surroundings. Our questions help us interpret our perceptions. Our focus questions needn't be complicated. They need only direct our attention to concern for the other person's spirit: Is he or she okay? What does this individual need? How does God love this person?

In the mid-1980s, Pope John Paul II was invited to meet with the Supreme Patriarch in Thailand. The protocol for the meeting required that before conversing, the two men would sit and regard each other for thirty minutes without talking. Imagine looking into the eyes of a stranger for thirty minutes before speaking. After a few moments of discomfort, you would start to notice the details: the lines of the face, the color of the eyes, the scars, blemishes, and sun spots. You would really see that person because you would be forced to pay attention. Compassion begins with paying enough attention to see the cares, needs, and crosses of another person.

Recently an old friend sent me an e-mail with two pictures attached. The first was a black-and-white image of a photographer. The second was a color picture of small child crawling across the ground of the African savanna; about twenty feet away was a vulture—just waiting. The accompanying text explained that the photographer had snapped this picture as the child made his way to a source of food. The image of the child was disturbing. It brought to mind a question posed by a college philosophy professor: If you are confronted with a situation that you believe ought not to happen, are you obligated to help?

Shortly after the photo was taken, the photographer returned to the United States. Six months later he committed suicide. One entry in his journal was a plea to God to let him never waste a single bit of food or forget to be grateful for the abundance he had.

The photographer's heartrending portrait of an African child crawling toward food paints a dramatic picture that can profoundly affect us, inspiring us to act with compassion. Surprising and vivid images like this one have the power to wake us up spiritually, while the more commonplace scenes we encounter every day—that ought to inspire the same compassion—evoke a different response. Why do we see the suffering in our own neighborhoods differently than that of a child in a faraway country? Do we use a different lens?

Jesus saw all people through the lens of compassion. He looked upon Jairus, the centurion, the lepers, the tax collectors, and the Syrophoenician woman with the same care and empathy. As Christians striving to live out the law of love, we have been both invited and instructed by Jesus to internalize this habit of seeing people in need through the lens of compassion. We focus this lens by asking ourselves the proper question. The next time you see someone in a situation you think ought not to exist, look with your heart as well as your eyes and ask yourself: *what does that person need?*

From Jesus Priority to Essential Habit

Practices for the 1st essential habit: Heal

- *stay deeply connected to compassion*
- *say yes to strangers*
- *do what is within our power to do*
- *see with the heart*

Reflect on the Gospel

When Jesus saw [Mary] weeping, and the Jews who came with her also weeping, he was deeply moved in spirit and troubled; and he said, "Where have you laid him?" They said to him, "Lord, come and see." Jesus wept. —John 11:32-34

Reflect on Your Priorities

How do you intentionally act with compassion?

How can you say yes to strangers?

Does somebody near you, or on the edges of your life, need compassion: what is within your power to do?

Think about someone you may have judged harshly. If you look again with your eyes and your heart, what do you see?

Prayer

Abba, help me stay deeply conscious of your compassionate love for people. Teach me to treat strangers no differently than family and to see all your children with compassionate eyes. Grant me the courage to do what is within my power to do. Amen.

JESUS PRIORITY 2

Love

GOSPEL STORY—*The Great Commandment*

One of them, a lawyer, asked him a question, to test him.
"Teacher, which is the great commandment in the law?" And
he said to him, "You shall love the Lord your God with all
your heart, and with all your soul, and with all your mind.
This is the great and first commandment. And a second is like
it, You shall love your neighbor as yourself. On these two
commandments depend all the law and the prophets."
—MATTHEW 22:35-40 (SEE ALSO DEUT. 6:5 AND LEV. 19:18)

MOST CHRISTIANS are familiar with this Gospel story of the Great
Commandment recounted above. When asked about the greatest commandment, the heart of the law, Jesus draws upon the prayer known to
all the Jews of his time: the Shema. "Hear, O Israel: The LORD our God
is one LORD; and you shall love the LORD your God with all your heart,
and with all your soul, and with all your might" (Deut. 6:4-5). While the
Gospels do not report Jesus quoting them, the verses directly following
the Shema also would have been well known by his contemporaries.

And these words which I command you this day shall be upon
your heart; and you shall teach them diligently to your children,
and shall talk of them when you sit in your house, and when you
walk by the way, and when you lie down, and when you rise. And

35

you shall bind them as a sign upon your hand, and they shall be as frontlets between your eyes. And you shall write them on the doorposts of your house and on your gates.—DEUTERONOMY 6:6-9

Clearly love of God and neighbor must be our constant concern, a mental guidepost for daily living. We can teach this principle to our children while we walk, while we play, when we lie down to sleep, and when we rise. The heart of God's law—loving God and others—must consume us. When we let love for others consume us, we come nearest to God. What is the nature of the love God wants us to share? It is not romantic love, sex, attraction, or desire. Jesus never spoke about these things. God's love, the love that Jesus proclaimed, concerns mercy.

God's loving mercy is an overarching message of Jesus' teaching. All the other priorities could rightly be classified under this theme. In his ministry and life Jesus modeled living according to love and the golden rule—the heart of God's law. Jesus spoke directly about love as the foundation of God's law in a number of circumstances by drawing upon the scriptures, contrasting them with contemporary life, and telling stories. These teachings can be grouped into three general categories: Show Mercy First; Forgive without Limit; and Love Others as God Loves.

SHOW MERCY FIRST

Mercy is one of the chief defining characteristic of the love that Jesus modeled for us. Jesus praises the virtue of mercy by proclaiming, "Blessed are the merciful" (Matt. 5:7). Some of his most poignant stories focus on the virtue of mercy, including the parable of the good Samaritan in Luke 10:29-37. When Jesus tells a lawyer that to inherit eternal life he should love God and love his neighbor, the lawyer asks, "And who is my neighbor?" Jesus recounts his story and concludes by asking which of the characters was a "neighbor" to the man who'd been attacked. The lawyer answers, "The one who showed mercy on him."

Jesus acknowledges the correctness of the response by saying, "Go and do likewise" (Luke 10: 25-37).

To appreciate the story, remember that Jews of that time viewed Samaritans as practicing corrupt religion; they were shunned and avoided. A Samaritan would generally not expect compassion if roles in the parable were reversed. The irony of the unclean Samaritan being the hero of the story would not have been lost on Jesus' listeners. Jesus makes it clear that God loves those who share his love with people in need, regardless of nationality, faith, or even prior sins. The act of being merciful brings us closer to God; anyone who becomes an agent of God's mercy pleases God.

Jesus' famous parable makes it clear that mercy comes first, superseding all other considerations. On four different occasions the Pharisees attacked Jesus and his followers for violating the laws of Judaism. According to these practices, healing on the Sabbath or picking grain in the fields on the Sabbath when they were hungry was considered work and a violation of the commandment to rest on the Sabbath day. Eating with sinners or failing to wash before eating would render them unclean and in need of purification. When challenged by the Pharisees at these times, Jesus responds forcefully, pointing out that these concerns for human ritual are not important to God. Jesus took advantage of these occasions to teach us that the heart of the law, not the letter of the law, is what matters most.

> Then he called the crowd to him and said to them, "Listen and understand: it is not what goes into the mouth that defiles a person, but it is what comes out of the mouth that defiles. . . . Do you not see that whatever goes into the mouth enters the stomach, and goes out into the sewer? But what comes out of the mouth proceeds from the heart, and this is what defiles. For out of the heart come evil intentions, murder, adultery, fornication, theft, false witness, slander. These are what defile a person, but to eat with unwashed hands does not defile."
> —Matthew 15:10-11, 17-20, nrsv

Beyond giving priority to mercy over ritual, Jesus did not comment on specific ritual practices during his public ministry. He certainly did not rail against rituals in their entirety but emphasized keeping first things first. Jesus' mission was to teach us that what matters most—loving others and loving God—must never be sacrificed for the things that matter less.

Rituals are a human creation, designed to bridge the mystery between heaven and earth, to reinforce and celebrate faith. They can be significant elements of personal and communal worship. But rituals are not faith, only signs of faith. When they become more important than or disconnected from the belief and faith they celebrate, they can actually hinder spiritual growth.

Jesus offers mercy because of who God is.

This emphasis on love and mercy over ritual during Jesus' public ministry provides us with some insight regarding his assertion that he did not come "to abolish [the law and the prophets] but to fulfil them" (Matt. 5:17). Jesus came to reveal the law, to clarify God's intent. Jesus came to fulfill the law by reminding us that God's law is simple and not dependent on ritual. By talking about and modeling love and mercy Jesus brought about a more complete understanding of God's law. By reflecting on and practicing the most fundamental commandments of God, we also can make God's commandment of love a reality.

Mercy—No Matter What

In the parable of the good Samaritan (Luke 10:29-37), the hero of the tale behaves in an extraordinary way. Jesus' listeners would have been stunned because they had no reason to assume the Samaritan in the story was any different than the average Samaritan—typically treated with disdain by the average Jew. No one would have been surprised if the Samaritan failed to be compassionate. And that is exactly why the story is moving: expectations are upended. The Samaritan does help, demonstrating that those who show mercy—regardless of their faith or heritage—are close to the heart God.

The ability to treat others with mercy regardless of how they treat us requires that our actions flow from principles, not circumstance. Being imperfect, we can sometimes allow the stimulus of anger, violence, or undesirable actions by others to dictate our own behavior. But we were not designed in the image of God to be reactive. We don't have to let circumstance or emotions determine our responses.

As children of God, we each possess three fundamental endowments with which God has blessed us: (1) a spirit fashioned in God's image, (2) the capacity to love, and (3) free will. We can consciously choose to be the agents of God's will. By accepting these gifts and using them for their intended purpose—loving others—we can learn to be merciful, no matter what.

Let's consider some of the justifications people offer for choosing not to be merciful and compare them with Jesus' perspective.

1. *They don't have the means.* Jesus didn't worry about financial means; most of those who received his mercy wanted something other than money anyway—like human compassion or even simple recognition.
2. *They don't have time.* Jesus never worried about time; he stopped to help each time he was asked.
3. *They fear judgment of others.* Jesus didn't worry about the social stigma of talking with or, heaven forbid, touching, the "wrong kinds of people." He saw those rules as hurtful, so he ignored them.
4. *They consider a merciful response undeserved.* Jesus knew that mercy is not earned like justice; it is a gift. Mercy is more than justice; mercy saves where justice might demand restitution or punishment.

Jesus teaches that mercy is offered not because of who the recipients are or even who we are. Jesus offers mercy because of who God is. Jesus never relinquished this mission of revealing the love of God to us. He offered mercy—no matter what.

FORGIVE WITHOUT LIMIT

The second quality of Christian love to which Jesus calls us is a forgiving heart. The story of the woman who washes Jesus' feet, recounted in all four Gospels, illustrates this theme of forgiveness.[1] It remains one of the most moving events in Jesus' public ministry. A woman "of the city" (implied to be a prostitute in Luke's version) rushes into the home of the Pharisee who has invited Jesus to dinner. She washes the feet of Jesus with her tears and dries them with her hair.

No act lies beyond forgiveness.

When the Pharisee is outraged, Jesus praises the woman's act of humility and love, then contrasts it with the poor hospitality shown to Jesus by his host. Jesus goes on, "Therefore I tell you, her sins, which are many, are forgiven, for she loved much."

Jesus tells this woman—and us—that our sins are forgiven when we love others with mercy, compassion, and humility. No act lies beyond forgiveness. Jesus extends mercy and forgiveness to this woman of the city, whose sins are many, and empowers her to change. In the same way, Jesus expects us to extend mercy and forgiveness to one another. This moral principle is echoed in a common tenet of the mental health disciplines: if you want people to change, you must first accept them the way they are. Jesus did exactly that; he accepted sinners and challenged them to change.

In April 2004 Archbishop Desmond Tutu spoke at the University of the Pacific in Stockton, California. Bishop Tutu served as the Anglican Archbishop of South Africa from 1986 to 1996. He was a marvel to see and hear, bringing peace by his very presence and drawing forth from each person in the room a sense of goodness and holiness with a smile that would not yield. He reflected on the ten-year anniversary of the fall of apartheid in South Africa and on the enormous change over that time for his people. He was joyful, excited that his country had been free for one decade. He shared insights regarding his involvement in the work of the Truth and Reconciliation Commission and the challenge of bringing healing and peace to people who had been mired in conflict for so long. He, more than most, profoundly understands the importance of forgiveness and spiritual healing.

During his comments, Bishop Tutu described a pivotal act by Nelson Mandela after Mandela's release from prison and election as president of South Africa. Mandela invited his jailer to stand beside him as his personal guest at his inauguration. Both Mandela and Tutu knew they needed to initiate the directive of Christ: love your enemies. Bishop Tutu praised Mr. Mandela for this decision, for the incredible extension of goodwill to one who had personally stood watch over Mandela's captivity. Nelson Mandela and Archbishop Tutu both recognized the only path that could free their country from decades of bitterness, hatred, and division: the path of love, forgiveness, and peace.

Bishop Tutu believes that all of us have this power of forgiveness. He spoke passionately about the good in each of us, an inherent goodness that both seeks and offers forgiveness. He promised us this: "There is nothing you can do to make God love you more. There is also nothing you can do to make God love you less."

God loves us perfectly, so the only way to improve our relationship with God and our ability to receive God's endless love is by improving things on our end. What can we do to love God more? We bring compassion, understanding, and forgiveness to those who are suffering.

Jesus Gave Us the Power to Forgive

On more than one occasion Jesus proclaimed, "Your sins are forgiven." Jesus shared this authority over sin with us, giving us the ability to forgive one another. That's an incredible gift as well as an awesome power and responsibility.

> "Whatever you loose on earth shall be loosed in heaven."
> —MATTHEW 16:19; 18:18

> "How often should I forgive? . . ." Jesus said to him, "Not seven times, but, I tell you, seventy-seven times."—MATTHEW 18:21-22, NRSV

"Whenever you stand praying, forgive."—MARK 11:25

"If there is repentance, . . . you must forgive him."—LUKE 17:3-4, NRSV

When Jesus healed, he often did so by forgiving the sins or celebrating the faith of those in need of healing. Note that when Jesus offers both, forgiveness precedes cure every time. By forgiving sins and affirming faith in God, Jesus freed those whom he healed. He released them as he proclaimed he would in Luke 4:18: "He has sent me to proclaim release to the captives." Forgiveness is essential for spiritual healing and so an essential part of love.

The adulterous woman incident (John 8:3-11) gives us perhaps the most instructive principle regarding forgiveness. The story is relatively simple: a woman is caught in the act of adultery and brought before Jesus to determine if she should be stoned to death. Her guilt is not in doubt. If Jesus says, "No, don't stone her," he'll be accused of defying Mosaic Law. If he says, "Yes, stone her," he'll be violating the very doctrine he preaches.

As he does in other situations where adversaries try to trip him up, Jesus sees past the false dilemma. The scribes and Pharisees do not truly want Jesus to judge this woman; they have already judged her. Rather, they seek to judge Jesus. Jesus turns their challenge back upon them: "Let him who is without sin among you be the first to throw a stone at her." Now faced with the question originally aimed at Jesus, the whole crowd is forced into some unscheduled self-reflection.

Gospel readers know Jesus has mentioned this principle before: "How can you say to your neighbor, 'Let me take the speck out of your eye' while the log is in your own eye?" (Matt. 7:4, NRSV). Jesus makes his point again with the woman's accusers but in a more poignant way. The lesson: before we are called to rebuke evil, we are first called to self-judgment.

Slowly the accusers drop their stones. In light of Jesus' challenge, no one could throw one, for claiming to be without sin would be an act of blasphemy. Jesus knew there could be only one response to his question. Surely the men in the crowd, in the silence of their minds, admitted to themselves that while they had not committed adultery, they'd been tempted. They'd had these thoughts, perhaps even looked for opportunity to act on their impulses or vices. When the crowd is gone, Jesus asks, "Woman, where are they? Has no one condemned you?"

"No one, Lord."

Jesus releases her with, "Neither do I condemn you; go, and do not sin again."

This story communicates that anyone and anything can be forgiven. Jesus calls us to extend our forgiveness to all who ask. The particular sin involved should not matter to us. Jesus gave us no instructions on which sins to forgive and which to condemn.

> Be on your guard! If another disciple sins, you must rebuke the offender, and if there is repentance, you must forgive. And if the same person sins against you seven times a day, and turns back to you seven times and says, "I repent," you must forgive.—LUKE 12:3-4, NRSV

Our willingness to forgive others is founded on our commitment to God and our desire to extend God's love. Forgiving our neighbors begins with our compassion and our humility—not others' mistakes. Their transgressions merely serve to remind us of our own humanity, our own imperfections. This is what Christ conveyed when he said, "first take the log out of your own eye." By recalling our own imperfections first, we can increase our humility and acknowledge our own desire to be forgiven. The strength to extend forgiveness comes from the power of understanding—understanding the human struggle against temptation's seductive lure. We all know this struggle; it is in each of us. We know when we've been strong. We know also when we've lost some battles—when we've needed forgiveness.

Jesus came to show us the nature of our loving and forgiving God. He extended forgiveness even to his jailers and executioners. This is the standard to which Jesus has called us. "You, therefore, must be perfect, as your heavenly Father is perfect" (Matt. 5:48). Part of that perfection means to be perfectly humble and perfectly forgiving.

When I was a teenager my parents once had an argument that was very . . . spirited. Voices were raised, and it got pretty uncomfortable. At one point one parent said, "I don't want to talk when you're angry."

The response: "I *want* to be angry!"

Each of us probably can identify with that sentiment. We don't want to hear apology or explanation until we are done being angry. Yet we often force young children to apologize immediately after they have hurt someone. I know I've made my children say "I'm sorry" to each other, even when one party or the other clearly was still recovering—still hurt or angry.

We play the role of the angry victim easily, giving voice to our condemnation of others. But that is not the model Jesus presented, and it is not the way we hope to be treated by God. That's why the Lord's Prayer contains this element of seeking forgiveness after we have forgiven. Recall Matthew 6:12: "forgive us our debts, as we also have forgiven our debtors." The translation doesn't read "Forgive me as often as—that is, to the extent that—I forgive others" but "forgive me because I have already forgiven others."

Finally, we must remember that forgiveness is only the beginning. We must move beyond forgiveness and work for reconciliation. Forgiveness means "granting pardon without harboring resentment," the resolution of conflict. Reconciliation is more. Jesus' call to "love your neighbor" challenges us to reconcile, to restore the relationship to its former status. Forgiveness is the first step. Reconciliation is the goal.

LOVE OTHERS AS GOD LOVES

The third fundamental truth about love revealed in Jesus' public ministry is that we are the chosen instruments of God's love. Jesus calls us to extend the Father's love. In Matthew 7:12 Jesus says, "In everything do to others as you would have them do to you; for this is the law and the prophets" (NRSV). Each of us wants to be loved, and so we are called to be a source of that love. This Golden Rule is so well known it transcends Christianity. It has such universal appeal and application to our lives that some consider it the most important of Christ's teachings.

In a story known as the judgment of the nations (Matt. 25:31-46), Jesus illustrates what will happen at the end of all things "when the Son of man comes in his glory, and all the angels with him, then he will sit on his glorious throne. Before him will be gathered all the nations, and he will separate them one from another as a shepherd separates the sheep from the goats." Those who have shown love, mercy, and compassion to those in need "inherit the kingdom prepared for you from the foundation of the world." Those who failed in this task are sent "into the eternal fire prepared for the devil and his angels." The "goats" are surprised and ask, "Lord, when did we see thee hungry or thirsty or a stranger or naked or sick or in prison, and did not minister to thee?" They are told, "Truly, I say to you, as you did it not to one of the least of these, you did it not to me."

The lesson of this story cannot be misinterpreted. Jesus' message is twofold: (1) all humans are worthy of and in need of God's love; and (2) all humans are accountable for offering God's love to others. Jesus' description of the return of the Son of Man reasserts the fact that we are created in God's image. God's spirit dwells within each of us. We touch that very holy part of ourselves when we extend God's love to anyone in need, touching God's spirit within others. We distance ourselves from God when we withhold love. This passage teaches us that the Golden Rule goes beyond "treat others as you would have them treat you." Here we realize that we are to treat others as God would treat them, or better, as we would have God treat us.

The Golden Rule intuitively makes sense for humans: model the behavior you expect from others. It makes sense because it seems fair. It raises questions though. Is God only as forgiving as we are? Does this mean if we do not love, we are doomed? Most of us do not love perfectly at all times, but neither do we completely fail at love. What will the gatekeeper do with those of us who are neither sheep nor goat? What if we love some of the time? We need to reconcile our imperfection with Jesus' warning "for with the judgment you pronounce, you will be judged" (Matt. 7:2).

Jesus knows we are not perfect, and he knows what it is like to be human. He gave us the model of his life to help us follow him in love.

But we lack his singular devotion to love; we lack his sense of perfect detachment from all the things of this world. Because of these deficiencies, we falter.

We looked at one remedy for this problem in chapter 2: Jesus gave us the power to forgive one another. After forgiveness, then what? The second remedy is a return to love. Jesus tells us: "Give for alms those things which are within; and behold, everything is clean for you" (Luke 11:41). Giving alms—an act of love through charity to someone in need who cannot respond in kind—restores us. It reconnects us with God's spirit within us and within others. When we love those who cannot return our mercy or generosity, when the extension of our love holds no promise of reciprocity or reward, then we love as God loves. Through the love of the stranger and the destitute we bring ourselves into deeper union with God.

> *Through the love of the stranger and the destitute we bring ourselves into deeper union with God.*

Love is the fundamental act God seeks from our freedom to choose. With our free will, we make all our decisions, choose our paths and our responses. We choose to accept the invitation of God. We choose love or apathy. When we choose not to love, there is only one hope: choosing to return to love.

The parable of the prodigal son (Luke 15:11-32) illustrates this truth. A son demands his share of his father's inheritance, leaves home, and foolishly squanders the money on loose living. After an economic downturn, he is reduced to feeding swine. Upon the son's return, the father is celebratory, not angry or punitive but celebratory. He rejoices in his son's return. When we falter, when we have chosen selfishly or unwisely, God will take us back. God rejoices in our return. God is always waiting for us, but we must turn toward God first. We turn back to God by returning to love, expressed in our ability to love others.

This chapter began with the Great Commandment: "You shall love the Lord your God with all your heart, and with all your soul, and with all your mind," and "You shall love your neighbor as yourself." Between these two famous quotations are five very important words which are often overlooked as a mere phrase to join these two ideas. They hold much more significance than that. The five words are: "And a second is like it" (Matt. 22:39). Jesus did not say, "That was number one, and here's number two." He did not say that the second was subordinate to the first. He did not mean that the one must be accomplished first, and only then should we pursue the second. He said, "And a second is like it." Jesus said that these two great commandments are really one and the same. We can't have one without the other. Treating others with compassion and mercy is our expression of love for God, just as contempt, hostility, or indifference toward others rejects the God of love. More than once Jesus told us "the tree is known by its fruit" (Matt. 12:33; Luke 6:44). As Saint John of the Cross wrote, "In the evening of life, they will examine thee in love."[2]

From Jesus Priority to Essential Habit

Practices for the 2nd essential habit: Love
- *show mercy no matter what*
- *forgive without limit*
- *love others as God loves*

Reflect on the Gospel

"In everything do to others as you would have them do to you; for this is the law and the prophets."—Matthew 7:12, NRSV

Reflect on Your Priorities

Who needs your mercy?

Who is the one person in your life with whom you would most like to be reconciled?

How can you create opportunities to give to those who cannot give back?

Prayer

Abba, help me to be a source of your mercy. Teach me to forgive others before I seek forgiveness for my own actions. Grant me the courage to extend your love to the stranger and the needy. Amen.

JESUS PRIORITY 3

Pray

Gospel Story—*Instruction on Prayer*

When you pray, you must not be like the hypocrites; for they love to stand and pray in the synagogues and at the street corners, that they may be seen by men. Truly, I say to you, they have received their reward. But when you pray, go into your room and shut the door and pray to your Father who is in secret; and your Father who sees in secret, will reward you.

—Matthew 6:5-6

During his public ministry, through word and deed, Jesus demonstrated the importance of prayer. Prayer was central to his mission as a means of nurturing his relationship with God and staying focused on God's will. Jesus was a pray-er. He prayed spontaneously and informally, matching his prayer to the moment. He encouraged others to pray and offered specific advice on how we can pray. Four patterns emerge from these passages. Jesus prayed alone, persistently, in the presence of others, and simply.

Pray Alone

While communal prayer holds a place in our faith life, we should not underestimate the critical role of private and personal prayer. Jesus apparently prayed alone regularly, and at least sometimes, these prayer sessions

49

were extended. "And in the morning, a great while before day, he rose and went out to a lonely place, and there he prayed" (Mark 1:35). And again: "In these days he went out to the mountain to pray; and all night he continued in prayer to God" (Luke 6:12).

Praying alone offers two obvious benefits. First, there are fewer distractions. Prayer takes concentration, and distractions only make the task more difficult. With the best of intentions we can so easily and so quickly become preoccupied with stray thoughts. In a seminar on professional communications skills, one presenter reminded his audience that others cannot "hear" us if they are hungry, distracted, in pain, or depressed. Likewise they cannot hear if they need to go to the bathroom, are worried about something or someone, or had a fight at home that morning. And the list goes on.

It takes work to shut out the distractions, to listen past the noise and the commotion of life. We have a much better chance of listening when we remove ourselves as much as possible from the din of activity all around us. By finding "a lonely place apart," we improve our chances of communicating better with God.

The second and larger benefit of praying alone is that false pretenses are not necessary. Praying alone ensures that neither our perceptions of others or our self-conscious concern for how others perceive us influence our prayer with God. When we are alone, it does not matter how we are dressed; God knows what we look like. It does not matter how well we sing, for no one else can hear, and God hears the song in our heart. The words we choose matter little, for God knows us deep in the silence of our soul, beyond words.

Spending time alone with God in prayer is essential. As we'll explore further, Jesus invites us into an intimate prayerful relationship with God. When we think of intimacy, notions of committed love spring to mind. When a couple is intimate, they share things that are special to them alone. Intimacy is not limited to physical intimacy, although that may be part of it. More important is the emotional and spiritual intimacy. When two people are intimate, they share with each other private thoughts, feelings, desires, fears, hopes. and dreams. It is this intimate communication between souls that sustains and deepens the relationship. These discussions are private; they are not conducted in the presence of others. When a sensitive subject arises in a public place, they protect the intimacy by saying, "Could I speak to you alone for a moment?"

Like these human relationships, our relationship with God also requires intimate moments of deep personal sharing. Such moments were precious to Jesus; he sought them out regularly. To be like him, we also must seek out these moments. Reaching ever deeper levels of intimacy is a solitary work. That's why we must commit ourselves to "finding our mountain" and going there often to pray alone with our God. There we can share our failures, our fears, and our hopes with God in intimate prayer.

Solitude beyond Prayer

The value of finding a "lonely place apart," as Jesus did, transcends prayer. Jesus sought out solitude. Before we listen to and talk with God in prayer, we need to spend time by ourselves in contemplation. What is contemplation? It is known by other names: meditation, reflection, introspection, self-analysis, and more. The term itself is unimportant. The point is that we need solitary time, independent of prayer, to focus inward.

Contemplation gives us time alone with our own thoughts. It is an exercise in considering our actions in light of our faith. It can be a time for sorting out how we feel and think about a concern and how to respond to it in the future. It is a time to reflect, considering what happened during the day, how we reacted, and the degree to which we met Jesus' standard of love. Solitary contemplation prepares us for prayer. During contemplation we assess ourselves. We take the results of our introspection to God in prayer.

An analogy from the world of education may be helpful. When teachers measure whether or not a child has mastered a skill or concept, they employ some kind of test. The child demonstrates her ability by completing an exam, writing an essay, or performing a task. One of the most revealing aspects of this process is to ask the child what she thinks her work demonstrates, what she's learned through the process, and how she knows she has learned it. Educators refer to this as *metacognition*, an awareness of our own thought processes. Like contemplation, it is self-reflective. Our prayer—that is, our relationship and communication with God—can be much richer when we prepare for our conversation by developing a self-reflective understanding of our actions, motives, and feelings.

As you explore your personal faith, begin by reflecting on how you spend time when you are alone. Time without the distraction of others provides an opportunity to nurture practices and interests that help you recall God is with you. What activities do you reserve for private moments? These choices critically affect your spiritual formation.

Humans are not perfect; we can have desires that are physically, mentally, or spiritually unhealthy. Pursuing these desires tempts us most when we are alone, because we usually prefer not to be seen feeding our vices. So we can be lulled into letting our spiritual guard down when others aren't around. That is why our conduct when we are certain no one else will learn of our behavior is a good measure of our integrity. Truly, it is when we are alone that we need to be strongest! Just as we must let our light shine for others to see, we also must keep our lamp lit for ourselves. We need to shine our faith inward. Being alone does not signal a time to let up but to light up. Burn your brightest when you are alone!

We need to shine our faith inward.

You can begin this work by practicing being truly alone. An hour with just you and your MP3 player does not count. Curling up with your favorite novel or watching a favorite television show may be valuable downtime, but in these situations you are not alone. You are *with* your music or *with* your show. To practice being alone—just you and your God—strive to remove all other distractions. Jesus went up on the mountain for a reason: to get away from the distractions all around him.

As you practice solitude and contemplation, a simple tool to aid your spiritual growth is a faith journal. Keep a written record of your spiritual quest. A writer once commented, "I don't know what I think until I see what I've said." Life is complicated, and spiritual matters are no less so; it's easy to talk or think ourselves into circles. Committing your thoughts, hopes, and beliefs to words on paper brings clarity and sometimes resolution to the questions and struggles. It also allows you to see over time that you actually are growing closer to God.

PRAY PERSISTENTLY

Jesus' praise for persistence in stories like the unjust judge (Luke 18:1-7) and the persistent friend (Luke 11:5-13) can be interpreted as a promise from Jesus that if we pray loud enough and often enough, God will give us what we want. This implies an image of God as a loving parent, who gives the children all that they ask for. That sounds nice, but it's a deceptive belief that can seriously damage our relationship with God by creating some false expectations within us.

A careful reading of the persistent friend story reveals an often-overlooked distinction fundamental to Jesus' teaching on prayer. The final verse says, "If you then, who are evil, know how to give good gifts to your children, how much more will the heavenly Father give the Holy Spirit to those who ask him!" (Luke 11:13). All the other statements Jesus made about God's response to our prayers must be reconciled with this promise. God can grant us what we ask if we ask for the right things. Jesus recommended we ask for the Holy Spirit. This is the persistence that Jesus wishes from us—an ongoing effort to discern God's will for our lives. He wants us to ask daily to be a channel of God's love, to be suffused with the Holy Spirit and guided by the Holy Spirit in all things.

In the late 1990s I heard a pastor in California tell a story about a young man's prayer that went something like this: The young man raised his eyes to heaven in prayer and said, "O God, grant me happiness."

God replied, "No. I give you blessings. Happiness is up to you."

The young man considered this and asked, "O God, take away my pride."

God answered, saying, "No. Your pride is not mine to take away; it is yours to give."

After a pause the man said, "God, help me grow."

"No," God responded. "I will not make you grow. I will prune you, so that you will bear fruit."

The young man persisted, "God, please spare me from pain."

"No," said God. "Pain draws you away from worldly cares and draws you closer to me."

The young man considered this and then tried again in earnest. "O God, take my handicapped child and make her whole."

God said to him, "No. Her spirit is whole. The body is only temporary anyway."

The young man asked God for all things that he might enjoy life. But God replied, "No. I gave you life, so that you might enjoy all things."

The man became frustrated and complained, "God? Don't you love me at all?"

And God assured him, "I do. I gave you my only Son, so that if you believed in him, you would have eternal life."

The man was quiet for a long time. He finally raised his voice once more in prayer and said simply, "God, help me to love others as much as you love me."

"Okay," said God, "You're finally getting it."

To adopt the behavior of praying persistently, we need to pray regularly—ideally every day. If you don't have this habit, start now. Give God ten seconds of your time right before you go to bed at night or when you first arise in the morning. Give God just ten seconds of quiet listening. Then add five seconds each day until you can give God a few minutes of quiet listening on a daily basis. Listen and talk to God every day.

PRAY IN THE PRESENCE OF OTHERS

Jesus prayed with and amidst his followers. Whether it was aloud or quietly to himself, Jesus prayed with ease. When he fed five thousand with the miracle of the loaves and fishes, Jesus "looked up to heaven and blessed" (Matt. 14:19). When he raised Lazarus from the dead, he prayed for the entire crowd to hear. Luke's Gospel records that after his public baptism in the Jordan River by John, he was praying. On an occasion when Jesus was praying in the presence of others, one of his disciples asked him to teach them how to pray (Luke 11:1). This disciple asked because they all knew from experience that Jesus prayed regularly and that it was important to him—an integral part of his identity, his mission, and his daily activity.

Listen and talk to God every day.

Two characteristics are noteworthy in these times when Jesus prays publicly. First, these prayers were not in the context of liturgy or formal worship. They occur in the context of his daily ministry; they were spontaneous responses to the circumstances around him. Second, when Jesus prayed publicly, he was not leading the people in prayer; he was not inviting them to participate. His prayers were his own personal prayers, offered in the presence of others. He wanted his prayers to be heard; he was revealing part of his faith to those around him by giving them a glimpse of his relationship with God. It was instructive and inspiring for his listeners to hear his prayer. It helped their faith.

Like Jesus, we too are called to share our faith. Praying in the presence of others can have a profound impact on those around us. Praying amid family and friends builds up the faith of each person. By serving as models to one another, we reinforce our belief in God and the importance of prayer. Praying with others also lifts us out of ourselves. Hearing the prayers of others helps us to see past our own personal needs, to see that in this life we are connected to other humans who need our compassion. Praying together changes our hearts and inspires us to individual or collective action.

Pray Simply

When his followers asked for instruction on prayer, Jesus taught them the Lord's Prayer (Matt. 6:9-13). Many of us learned this prayer in our youth in Sunday school or church. It is often invoked in community prayer situations, and it allows people of different Christian denominations to pray together. Jesus, though, offered it as an example of personal prayer. In Matthew, he introduces it right after saying, "When you pray, go in to your room and shut the door and pray to your Father" (Matt. 6:6). Alone in our room with our God, who doesn't need us to "heap up empty phrases as the gentiles do" (Matt. 6:7), we can speak plainly to the Lord.

Jesus was instructing us in something more than formal, memorized prayer. He offered the Lord's Prayer to illustrate the kind of prayer to strive for, the kind of relationship to build with our God. Jesus kept it simple. Prayer doesn't have to be long or formal to be acceptable to God. Jesus showed us that content, not packaging, is what counts. Consider the message behind the words of the Lord's Prayer. Then make up your own prayer in your own words. You do not have to write it down. Remember: keep it simple.

Our Father ...

Enter into intimate prayer with God. Jesus told us to do this, and he demonstrated it. He invited us to approach God, his Father, as God, our Father. We are invited to approach Abba in prayer like a child in an affectionate relationship with a loving parent. This intimacy carries with it the promise of deep personal knowledge of one another. When we are intimate with someone, that person learns all about us. We share the most private and vulnerable part of ourselves. Like a spouse, an intimate knows the desires of our heart and can tell when we prevaricate. Efforts to conceal part or all of our actions and thoughts don't work, because the other knows us. The person understands our nature and has seen our vices and attempts to conquer them. This is the intimate relationship we can establish with God.

who art in heaven,
Hallowed be thy name ...
Like the tax collector who is afraid to lift up his eyes to heaven in Luke 18:9-14, enter into prayer in humility. A quick reflection on who we are

should lead us naturally to humility when we approach the One who made the earth and stars and all living things. This reverence and praise for God does not separate us from God but draws us closer. And your praise for God needn't be ritualized or formal, just sincere.

> *Thy kingdom come,*
> *Thy will be done,*
> *On earth as it is in heaven...*

"Seek first his kingdom and his righteousness," Jesus said (Matt. 6:33). Prayer is not about telling God what you want to accomplish but learning what God wants you to accomplish. In prayer, listen to discern God's will; ask for the strength to act.

This part of the prayer is a promise we make to God. It proclaims our intent to bring God's will to fruition through us, implicitly committing to go out and live the prayer. We will work to bring about God's will. We promise to become a vessel for God's purposes.

After we listen to discern God's will, we need to go do it. Some pursue prayer in the hopes that it will bring them peace, but that's not where Jesus found it. Jesus found peace by going outside himself. He taught us that when we put our concern for others first, when we act to serve their needs and heal their suffering, we let go of all the inner noise of our ego, our wants, our desires. Peace comes from living for others.

That is why the heart of Christian faith is not found solely in the solitude of personal prayer and reflection. We pray for the strength to build God's kingdom. Then we need to get to work building the kingdom. Jesus showed us that prayer is meant to connect us with God's vision for our lives and strengthen our will to work toward that vision.

Give us this day our daily bread ...

Bread was a staple in Jesus' day, an essential part of the meal. The Jews relied upon it for their sustenance. Jesus' reference to bread sounds simpler than it is. In reflecting on prayer, people often will quote Jesus' promise in John 16:23: "Very truly, I tell you, if you ask anything of the Father in my name, he will give it to you" (NRSV). But we need to ask for the right things: the Holy Spirit. What we often ask for is not "bread"—the essential we need—but what we want. Jesus never asked for what he wanted.

To pray like Jesus, ask for that which sustains and gives life: the capacity to love others. Ask to understand God's will for you and to be a part of God's plan; this you will receive.

Prayer is not for God's benefit but for ours; *we* need the prayer. The purpose of prayer is to understand God's will and to gain the strength to do it. Its purpose is for us to receive God's wisdom, not for God to receive ours. Prayer changes us. Prayer changes our hearts, transforms us from the inside out. This conversion of heart restores us to spiritual health.

And forgive us our debts, as we also have forgiven our debtors ...

As we have seen earlier, love as forgiveness was fundamental to Jesus' ministry. Enter into prayer with a heart that bears no ill will, carries no grudge. Jesus gave us the power to forgive one another. He directed us to do this. So before we enter into prayer, we need to forgive in our hearts those who have hurt us.

Once we have forgiven others, we enter into prayer and ask God to forgive us. This is critical for our spiritual well-being. If we never verbalize that we have committed sins in thought, word, or deed, we can deceive ourselves into believing we have not sinned. We let our sin fade from memory and pretend that we did not do these things. We falsely hope that time will erase our transgressions. With God, though, it just is not possible to ignore what is in our heart.

Pray for God to grant the mercy you have shown others, to treat you as you have treated others. If you are having trouble forgiving others, pray for the ability to do so.

And lead us not into temptation,
But deliver us from evil.

Jesus drove out many unclean spirits. He called them by name. He spoke specifically about evil and warned us against temptation. In prayer call your temptations by name. Remember that your prayer with God is intimate. God knows you, and you trust God. Talk about your temptations. Admit to yourself, in prayer with God, that they are there, and ask for help in overcoming those temptations.

Jesus offered the Lord's Prayer as a model for us, to demonstrate the elements of good prayer. We must learn to listen and talk to God like Jesus: without a script. Remember Jesus' simple outline: Intimacy, Praise, Humility, Seek God's Kingdom, Daily Bread, Forgiveness, and Temptations. The order is not important; mix them up if you like, and you don't have to do all of them every time.

A Sample Prayer Using Jesus' Guidelines

Intimacy:	Abba, it's me, (*your name*).
Praise and Humility:	Great is your name! Wonderful is your creation!
Seek God's Kingdom:	Please, help me understand your will for my life. *Pause to listen.*
Daily Bread:	Send me your Holy Spirit to sustain me. *Pause to listen.*
Forgiveness:	I have been angry with (*name*) and need help in forgiving (*name*). *Pause to listen.* I ask your forgiveness for (*something specific*).
Avoid Temptations:	I'm really struggling with (*a specific temptation*). Please help me to be strong. *Pause to listen.*

From Jesus Priority to Essential Habit

Practices for the 3rd essential habit: Pray
- *pray alone*
- *pray persistently*
- *pray in the presence of others*
- *pray simply*

Reflect on the Gospel

If you then, who are evil, know how to give good gifts to your children, how much more will the heavenly Father give the Holy Spirit to those who ask him!—Luke 11:13

Reflect on Your Priorities

Where is your "mountain" for being alone with God?
How can you protect time for prayer in your daily routine?
How can you cultivate ongoing opportunities to pray with others?
What are some ways you can keep your prayer life simple?
In prayer how much are you listening?

Prayer

Abba, help me to find the solitude I need in you. Teach me to seek you constantly and to learn your will. Teach me how to pray with others. Grant me the simplicity to talk with you honestly about my struggles. Amen.

JESUS PRIORITY 4

Spread the Word

GOSPEL STORY—*The Call of Peter*

As he walked by the Sea of Galilee, he saw two brothers, Simon who is called Peter and Andrew his brother, casting a net into the sea; for they were fishermen. And he said to them, "Follow me, and I will make you fishers of men." Immediately they left their nets and followed him. And going on from there he saw two other brothers, James the son of Zebedee and John his brother, in the boat with Zebedee their father, mending their nets, and he called to them. Immediately they left the boat and their father, and followed him.

—MATTHEW 4:18-22 (SEE ALSO MARK 1:16-20)

THIS PRIORITY remains at the heart of Jesus' mission on earth. All the healing and preaching were part of his larger goal to reveal God's love to the world. He had Good News, and he wanted to spread the word. In the two thousand years since his earthly life among us, Jesus' message has been received by millions. Millions more still need to hear it. Jesus told us that "the harvest is plentiful, but the laborers are few" (Matt. 9:37; see also Luke 10:2). Jesus is relying on us to continue that work. How can we do that? Jesus' strategies for spreading the word were effective and replicable:

- share the mission
- invite everyone
- challenge with love

61

Share the Mission

Jesus did not see the task of preaching the good news as his alone; he sought out and welcomed help in that mission. He invited many to follow him, usually one at a time or in small groups, as in the story above, where he catches Simon, Andrew, and the sons of Zebedee with a single net. From the many who followed him, our Lord appointed twelve apostles (Matt. 10:1-4; Mark 3:14-19; Luke 6:12-16) to work alongside him. After a time, he sent the twelve out on their own ahead of him (Matt. 10:5, 7; Mark 6:7-12; Luke 9:1-2) to "preach the kingdom God and to heal" (Luke 9:2). Luke's Gospel tells us that Jesus commissioned seventy others to go forth with the instruction "Whenever you enter a town and they receive you, eat what is set before you; heal the sick in it and say to them, 'The kingdom of God has come near to you'" (Luke 10:8-9).

Jesus didn't share his mission only with the followers that he handpicked. When a man who wanted to follow Jesus asked if he could go and bury his father first, Jesus answered him, "Leave the dead to bury their own dead; but as for you, go and proclaim the kingdom of God" (Luke 9:60). When his disciples forbade a stranger who was casting out demons in Jesus' name, Jesus told them that was a mistake: "Whoever is not against us is for us" (Mark 9:40, NRSV; compare Matt. 12:30 and Luke 11:23).

Jesus drove the many demons named Legion from the man in the Gadarenes. Once healed, the man wanted to accompany Jesus. "But Jesus refused, and he said to him, 'Go home to your friends, and tell them how much the Lord has done for you.'. . . And he went away and began to proclaim in the Decapolis how much Jesus had done for him, and everyone marveled" (Mark 5:19-20, NRSV).

Consider Jesus' opinion of John the Baptist. John appeared in the wilderness near the Jordan, preaching "Repent, for the kingdom of heaven is at hand" (Matt. 3:2). No miracles are attributed to John. He did not heal the sick, raise the dead, walk on water, or feed thousands. He only preached and baptized. Of his herald, Jesus said, "Among those born of women none is greater than John" (Luke 7:28).

Jesus invited others to help in proclaiming the kingdom. He specifically directed both his closest friends and strangers to spread the word.

INVITE EVERYONE

This lesson of invitation is well taught by the parable of the great banquet (Matt. 22:1-10; Luke 14:15-24). Some who are invited to the banquet excuse themselves because they are busy: "I have bought a field, and I must go out and see it; I pray you, have me excused." In response the householder sends his servants out: "Go out quickly to the streets and lanes of the city, and bring in the poor and maimed and blind and lame." When there are still seats left, he commands his servant, "Go out to the highways and hedges, and compel people to come in, that my house may be filled."

People often take from this parable the lesson that everyone is invited to God's banquet table. While this is true, another dimension of the story emerges when we consider who is doing the inviting: the king's servants. The parable of the great banquet leads us—also servants of the master—to continue the work that Jesus proclaimed at the beginning of his ministry:

> The Spirit of the Lord is upon me, because he has anointed me to preach good news to the poor. He has sent me to proclaim release to the captives and recovering of sight to the blind, to set at liberty those who are oppressed, to proclaim the acceptable year of the Lord.—LUKE 4:18-19

In this passage from Luke's Gospel, Jesus applies to himself the words of Isaiah. Jesus is anointed to serve. He was selected to "preach good news to the poor." Like him, the servants in the parable are instructed to gather all they can find, both "bad and good" according to Matthew. The householder alone, God, judges whether or not those who arrive are fit for the banquet. The servants do not judge; they have not been given that authority. They simply invite; that is their charge.

To respond to this directive of Christ, we too are asked to invite others to the kingdom. Accepting the call of Christ does not mean simply that we have been invited to the banquet. It means we accept the task of inviting others as well. We take up the role of the servant, of extending God's invitation to others to join in the great banquet. As Saint Teresa of Ávila said, "Jesus has no hands or feet on earth now but yours." It is our task to play the role of the servant. In following Jesus, we become stewards to the householder who hosts the great banquet, the feast of life. We are bound to extend his invitation by serving as vessels of his love, his mercy, and his compassion.

Why Inviting Others Is Hard

When I was about seventeen, I was walking in the shopping mall one day. As I passed the center of the mall, a young man about my age called to me, "Excuse me, do you know how to get to heaven?" His tone made it clear he wasn't asking for his own benefit but mine. I was already suspicious.

"Yes, I think I do."

"How?" he pressed.

"Well, I think you follow the commandments that Jesus gave us."

"That's right. Will you get down on your knees and thank the Lord right now for saving you?" His eyes were on fire with earnest intensity.

"No." I really did not want to kneel down in the shopping mall with a stranger and pray. I was afraid people would think I was strange. Most probably would have. I disengaged and walked away.

On another occasion my older sister and I were in the same shopping mall, and a young man called to us, "Come here." At first we thought he was calling to someone else. When I looked back after he yelled a second time, it was obvious that he was talking to us.

"Hey, stop! Come here!"

"Just keep walking," I told my sister as I grabbed her arm to hasten our pace.

"Hey!" he yelled, beginning to follow us. Soon he was jogging. It became clear we were not going to get away. As he approached us I stopped and turned, drawing a deep breath, adrenaline filling my arms and legs. I was preparing for confrontation.

He extended his hand to offer a prayer card. "Jesus loves you, man." I accepted the card, and he smiled and walked away.

"Thank you." I was too stunned to say anything else.

In retrospect, all these years later, I can appreciate the zeal of these young men. Truly their invitation was not much different than the one John the Baptist extended. But while their intention and effort were admirable, ultimately they were unproductive. Instead of evangelizing me, they scared me. This raises an important issue for us to consider. Many of us don't feel comfortable being excessively demonstrative about our faith in public or with strangers. That is not a failing; being aggressive with strangers will probably frighten people off rather than bring them closer. As a dear friend once told me, "People will not suffer being dragged by the heels to God." What then are good guidelines for extending Jesus' invitation?

Based on Jesus' model:

1. Be the manifestation of God's love to people.
2. Invite everyone.
3. Don't worry about what people think of you.

The approach Jesus used was comforting, because his invitation to God's love was deeply connected to healing, forgiveness, and compassion. Jesus' invitations were intertwined with his service to others. His love and his connection to God were so compelling that people sought Jesus out. To them, and all who would listen, he spoke constantly about God without regard for how he was perceived by others. Jesus didn't worry about how his message was received; he was smart enough to know that some would listen and learn, and some would call him crazy. Like the stewards in the parable of the great banquet, Jesus just kept inviting everyone: the disciples, the lepers, the centurions, the Samaritans, the tax collectors, and the prostitutes.

We need to worry less about what others think of us and more about how Jesus perceives us. Like Jesus, first and foremost we are to manifest

God's love to others. Love and compassion are powerful marketing tools for the Lord; people are drawn toward God's love. We share with them the stories of our faith and our lives that reveal the motive behind our actions. Then we invite them to join us.

A Dedication to Jesus' Gospel

Reading and studying the Gospels is central to spreading the good news Jesus gave us. Jesus is the way to God; he told us that. One of the best ways to know Jesus is to read his story. Drawing closer to God, deepening our spirituality, requires an intimate knowledge of the gospel of Jesus. We need to be deeply familiar with Jesus' life and ministry. Jesus said, "It is the spirit that gives life, the flesh is of no avail; the words that I have spoken to you are spirit and life" (John 6:63). That's true; Jesus' words are spirit and life. So, staying close to his gospel story should be a staple for life in God. In the chapter on prayer, I recommended spiritual contemplation as an important element of spiritual growth. When we engage in this self-reflective thought, we need a standard. We cannot assess ourselves in a vacuum; we need an external benchmark against which to measure our performance. For Christians, that standard is the gospel of Jesus.

While the Hebrew scriptures are filled with God's wisdom, as disciples of Jesus, we begin with the Gospels. Consider the relationship between Jesus and the Hebrew scriptures. Jesus was regarded by many in his day as the Messiah, the "anointed one" expected to save Israel and restore the Jews to their former glory. Within the framework of this belief, it makes sense that the evangelists, and especially believers from the Jewish tradition, would attempt to show the connections between Jesus and the faith teachings of the Hebrew scriptures. They understood Jesus to be the fulfillment of scriptural prophecy.

The poems, songs, stories, and history of the Hebrew scriptures can help us meditate on Christ's teachings. The story of God's love for us begins there and can provide insight into the history of the message Christ came to complete. The scriptures are filled with stories and teachings that illuminate the gospel of Jesus. They are a treasure of faith literature. What we're probing in this book, though, is the wisdom of Jesus.

When you rise each morning, commit to learning more about Jesus—not merely *read* about Jesus but *learn* about Jesus. Reading can be performed rather mechanically. Learning requires us to read for deep understanding. We must treasure the Gospels as we would a love letter from Christ or the biography of a beloved family member. Read the Gospels carefully. Pray and think about Jesus' life, teachings, parables, healings, miracles, and prayers. The result will not be knowing *about* Jesus but really *knowing* Jesus. Pray for insight into the truth beyond the text.

This attention to Jesus' life is an ongoing challenge. As we grow and our life circumstances change, we perceive the Gospels differently, interpreting and understanding them in new ways. The Gospels really are the living Word of God. They are alive to us because we are alive to them, and God's spirit is alive in us. The living Word of God speaks to God's living spirit within each of us. As long as we're living, we're changing; so the gospel of Jesus never grows old. It constantly renews itself to us. To put it more precisely, we are constantly renewed by it.

Do you have a copy of the Gospels that you really like? If not, go to the bookstore and find a translation that works for you. The particular translation is significant only to the extent that you find it readable and engaging.

Reading the Gospels is not difficult. It takes time and effort; that is all. To ensure that you do read them, you can establish a routine. A good metric for measuring whether or not you're reading the Gospels enough is the condition of your Bible. Is the binding creased? Are your favorite parts earmarked? Do you have questions written in the margins? Are any pages torn? Does it look *used*? What makes the book holy is the message it contains for us, not the paper or binding. Jesus left his story for us to read and reflect on; he really wants us to use our Bibles. If the Bible holds a place of honor in the house but is never opened, how much honor has it really been given?

CHALLENGE WITH LOVE

The concept of challenge is illuminated in the story of the rich man, recorded by Matthew (19:16-22), Mark (10:17-22), and Luke (18:18-23). A rich man approached Jesus asking what he must do to inherit eternal life. Jesus tells him to keep the commandments. The man responds, "I have done all these. What else do I lack?" By asking this in public, he must have been confident that Jesus' answer would be complimentary, validating his good behavior and good standing among his peers. Perhaps he was hoping Jesus would say, "You follow all the commandments? Great. Just keep it up and your place in heaven is assured."

Jesus surprises him with his answer, "If you would be perfect, go, sell what you possess and give to the poor, and you will have treasure in heaven; and come, follow me." Jesus' answer to the rich man is both good and bad news for us. First, the bad news: we are the rich man. If you are reading this book, you very likely live in a first world, industrialized, and economically stable country. We live like royalty compared to the majority of the world's population. Most of us know where our next meal is coming from, and we have more stuff than we need to live. As for Americans, even though our population represents only a fraction of the world population, we own a majority of the world's wealth and consume a majority of its resources. From our abundance, there is much more that we could do, and there is much more that needs to be done.

> *God did not send Jesus to solve all our problems.*

The good news is Jesus loves the rich man. Mark records that Jesus "looking upon him loved him" (Mark 10:21). This mans follows the law; he honors his parents. He is a good man. Jesus knows it's not easy to be perfect, though he does call us to perfection. He accepts us as we are, and then he calls us to be all that we were created to be. In his encounter with the rich man, Jesus offers a challenge that only Jesus could offer because he is perfect. Who else could issue such a challenge with any credibility?

Challenging others is hard because we must hold ourselves accountable to any standards or goal with which we challenge others. We must first judge ourselves, removing "the log out of your own eye, and then you will see clearly to take the speck out of your brother's eye" (Matt. 7:5). Whenever we dare to challenge others, we open ourselves up to criticism from others for failing to be perfect.

The problem is this: we are not like Jesus, so we are not going to be perfect. We are humans made in the image God, so we have a sense of what perfection might look like, but we are not capable of attaining that perfection. The best we can hope for is never to resign ourselves to our imperfections but to work constantly to improve ourselves.

Those we confront may ask, "Who are you to be casting stones?" Our imperfections must not prevent us from pointing out the actions of others that are troublesome. If we let that stop us, then no one would ever correct anyone. Ideally our imperfections generate compassion that ensures we put forth any challenge for the right reasons and in an appropriate way. Our intent is not to embarrass others. We do not seek to hurt them but to help them. True, leading a life of good example can be a quiet but effective way of productively encouraging better behavior in others. Sometimes, though, Jesus and God may need us to be a bit more direct. Challenging others is an expression of concern motivated by love and compassion. Our actions must be preceded by self-judgment, communicated with love and compassion, and offered with the knowledge that we invite challenge upon ourselves.

Sharing the mission, inviting people, and challenging people are three behaviors that Jesus modeled for us. How do we achieve these practically in our daily lives? About fifteen years ago, somewhere in the Midwest, a train conductor looked out ahead of his train and saw two toddlers on the railroad tracks. He immediately ordered the brakes thrown, but he already knew the train would not stop in time. He climbed out onto the front of the engine. At the last possible second, he leaped forward onto the tracks in front of the still-moving train and wrapped his arms around the children, pulling them down onto the tracks as the train passed over them. Miraculously, they survived. He was considered a real hero—and for good reason.

In an interview just days after the event, he was asked, "How do you feel?"

He answered, "Are you kidding? I feel great! Not because I was brave—it's not that. I just did what I thought had to be done. But if I never do anything worthwhile for the rest of my life, I have those two kids. Whatever they can make of their lives, I can share in that."

In moments like the train conductor experienced, what is required of us is absolutely clear. Unfortunately, for most of us, the call to spread the word is less dramatic and usually less obvious. Moses received explicit instructions from God. The apostles were told to follow Jesus and directed by him to preach the good news. These men knew without a doubt what they were supposed to do.

We also have been told. We have been given marching orders. That's why Jesus came—to tell us and show us what do to. He gave us clear direction. His instructions are few in number, simple in theory, and extremely demanding in practice. He wants us to spread the word.

From Jesus Priority to Essential Habit

> **Practices for the 4th essential habit: Spread the Word**
> *share the mission*
> *invite everyone*
> *challenge with love*

Reflect on the Gospel

Then Jesus told his disciples, "If any want to become my followers, let them deny themselves and take up their cross and follow me."—Matthew 16:24 (see also Mark 8:34; Luke 9:23)

Reflect on Your Priorities

Who have you invited to join God's kingdom? Who will you invite next?
What are some ways you could share your mission to be a disciple of Jesus? Who could you tell? What could you write?
Who in your life needs to be challenged? How can you confront that person with love and humility?

Prayer

Abba, give me the grace to invite others to your banquet. Help me always to deepen my understanding of the gospel of your Son. Grant me the wisdom to judge myself rightly and to challenge others compassionately. Amen.

JESUS PRIORITY 5

Build Up Treasure in Heaven

Gospel Story—*The Rich Fool*

And he said to them, "Take care! Be on your guard against all kinds of greed; for one's life does not consist in the abundance of possessions." Then he told them a parable: "The land of a rich man produced abundantly. And he thought to himself, 'What should I do, for I have no place to store my crops?' Then he said, 'I will do this: I will pull down my barns and build larger ones, and there I will store all my grain and my goods. And I will say to my soul, "Soul, you have ample goods laid up for many years; relax, eat, drink, be merry."' But God said to him, 'You fool! This very night your life is being demanded of you. And the things you have prepared, whose will they be?' So it is with those who store up treasures for themselves but are not rich toward God."

—Luke 12:15-21

THE STORY of the rich fool, a compelling parable, is one of twelve events about treasure in heaven recorded twenty-five times in the Gospels. Jesus' statements and stories about money, material possessions, and devotion to God include other famous passages: the stories of the pearl of great price, the hidden treasure, paying taxes to Caesar, and the widow's offering. Together, these stories reveal three goals to strive for: detachment, an abundance mentality, and justice.

73

DETACH FROM EARTHLY POSSESSIONS

Detachment is one of the paramount virtues Jesus conveys in his parables. He taught us that earthly treasure—the material wealth that often preoccupies us—has no spiritual value. Money and gold are simply mediums of exchange; they can be used for good or ill. As resources they can become the means to achieving justice and charity. Jesus told us that "you cannot serve God and mammon" (Matt. 6:24) and that "it is easier for a camel to go through the eye of a needle than for someone who is rich to enter the kingdom of God" (Mark 10:25, NRSV). These teachings make his position clear. Jesus hopes for us to find treasure in heaven; earthly possessions can prevent us from discovering that treasure. The stories of the hidden treasure and the pearl of great price in Matt. 13:44-45 both convey Jesus' instructions for securing heaven's treasure: give up everything else.

Brother Lawrence was a seventeenth-century French monk whose collected advice has been published in *The Practice of the Presence of God.* In these writings he describes well his attempt to follow Jesus' advice in his quest to become "God's alone." He counseled, "for love of him, renounce every thing that is not him, and begin to live simply as if there were no one in the world except him and you."[1]

To gain this hidden treasure, we must let go of other concerns; we must detach ourselves from their embrace. Detachment has been the concern of many great Christians. Saint Neilos the Ascetic, a fifth-century Orthodox saint and pupil of Saint John Chrysostom, wrote *Ascetic Discourse.* He described the challenge is this way:

> Those who travel by sea, when overtaken by a storm, do not worry about their merchandise but throw it into the waters with their own hands, considering their property less important than their life. Why, then, do we not follow their example, and for the sake of the higher life despise whatever drags our soul down to the depths? Why is fear of God less powerful than fear of the sea?

> In their desire not to be deprived of this transitory life, they
> judge the loss of their goods no great disaster; but we, who claim
> to be seeking eternal life, do not look with detachment on even
> the most insignificant object, but prefer to perish with the cargo
> rather than be saved without it.[2]

In Saint Neilos's story, the immediacy of their predicament inspires those on the ship. Let us suppose that we did have this sense of spiritual urgency. Even then, tossing our belongings over the bow of our lives will not achieve what we must accomplish. Purging ourselves of possession alone will not save us. Detachment is not poverty.

The fifteenth-century author of *The Imitation of Christ*, Thomas à Kempis, explained the challenge of detachment well when he wrote, "He who only shuns them outwardly, and does not pluck out their roots, will profit little."[3] Simply put, having things does not block our way to God, but wanting things does. If we deny ourselves pleasures or comforts but still earnestly desire them, little spiritual progress has been made. Detachment means to stop wanting. We must discipline our mind and spirit not only to no longer rely on material things for happiness but to no longer regard them at all.

This does not mean that money is evil; it isn't. We need to eat, to secure shelter, to take care of our family, to save for emergencies. We're not expected to impoverish ourselves, and we do need to be good stewards of the resources we have. Jesus doesn't warn against having them; he warns against relying on these material things for comfort, happiness, or peace. They are dangerous only when they become overly important to us.

In the story of the rich fool, Jesus helps us to see that worrying excessively about our assets prevents our being concerned with more significant, spiritual matters. Why is this a man a fool before God? For all his wealth, he has failed to discern and pursue the only thing of real worth: life in God. His attachment to material possessions blinds him to his spiritual poverty. If the rich man had not built bigger barns, what could he have accomplished? Could he have shared his good fortune, been more generous with his blessings?

In order for us to avoid the mistake of the rich fool we can take to heart the Lord's instruction to Catherine of Siena. In her writings Catherine records God's word to her during one of her visions: "the heart is a vessel that cannot remain empty. As soon as you have emptied it of all those transitory things you loved inordinately, it is filled . . . with gentle heavenly divine love that brings you to the water of grace."[4]

MAINTAIN AN ABUNDANCE MENTALITY

We can work toward detachment by developing an abundance mentality. An abundance mentality means "there is enough." People who possess this virtue see their glass half-full even though their glass may be very small. Regardless of how little they have, there is always enough to share. Jesus demonstrated an abundance mentality when he fed the five thousand people. This wonder made an intense and lasting impression, earning the distinction of being the only miracle recorded in all four Gospels (Matt. 14:13-21; Mark 6:32-44; Luke 9:10-17; John 6:1-15). The evangelists all agree on the following:

> Thousands were hungry.
> Jesus took five loaves of bread and two fish.
> Jesus prayed in thanks to God.
> He distributed the food so that all ate their fill.
> There were a dozen baskets full of leftovers.

Jesus taught us that if we share, if we combine our resources with trust in God, there is enough—the abundance mentality.

This perception that there is enough connects directly to our willingness to share compassionately. It flows naturally from being detached from our possessions; when we want less, we have enough. When we want or think we need more, there is never enough. Consider how Jesus praises the generosity of the poor widow in Mark 12:32-34:

And a poor widow came and put in two copper coins, which make a penny. And [Jesus] called his disciples to him, and said to them, "Truly, I say to you, this poor widow has put in more than all those who are contributing to the treasury. For they all contributed out of their abundance; but she out of her poverty has put in everything she had, her whole living."

This is why the poor are blessed. They have little and do not grow attached to what they do not possess. They learn not to crave more. They often have found contentment and peace in the little they possess. While the poor may have needs and wishes, they do not rely on their fulfillment for spiritual satisfaction. They understand need and learn compassion, share what little they have, and can actually develop an abundance mentality. There is always something that can be shared.

People with more wealth have choices to make. The more resources they have, the more opportunities they have to give or to withhold. Many people of wealth actually develop a scarcity mentality. There isn't enough. They could invest more for retirement or could maximize their cash flow. The more they have, the harder it seems to achieve the right balance. Sustaining an abundance mentality requires us to assume there is enough and to be consumed by compassion rather than acquisition. An abundance mentality results in finding peace through generosity rather than through ownership.

Jesus taught us that if we share, . . . there is enough.

The abundance mentality challenges our notions of fairness. But what is "fair"? A conventional answer would be "everybody gets the same" or "everybody gets what they earn." That standard may work for children on the playground dividing up a bag full of candy. For adults trying to discern a path of adult Christian living, "everybody gets the same" reflects an underdeveloped concept of fairness. Jesus offered us a different paradigm. As his disciples, we must learn a new definition of fairness: everybody does what they can, and everybody gets what they need.

As I sit in my backyard reworking this section of the book, my daughter—six years old—says, "Daddy, what are you doing out there?"

"I am working on my book."

"What is your book about?" she asks.

"It's about Jesus."

"Oh, nice. What words are you using?"

I explain that I am trying to teach others what *fair* means; some say fair means "everybody gets the same," but Jesus says fair means "everybody gets what they need." I use the example of two people. I say: "One is hungry and one is not. We have only one apple. Do we split the apple so both get half? Give the whole apple to the person who is not hungry and nothing to the person who is? Or give the whole apple to the person who is hungry and nothing to the person who is not?"

She passes the quiz, and says, "Daddy, I will make up a story for your book about *fair*. Everyone went to the festival to have a hot dog. And everybody got one. Except for one person who came there last. And the hot dogs were all gone. I came up and splitted my hot dog, and I gave them one half and we ate the hot dog together. Do you like that?"

"It's perfect."

As my four-year-old son opens the screen door to join us on the back patio, my daughter calls, "Nicky, c'mon. Me and daddy are writing a book about sharing and giving on the computer."

Why Being Fair Is Not Easy

Fair in Jesus' terms is difficult, because we have a tendency to believe we deserve what we have, that we earn our possessions. We extend this argument to those who have less: they did not earn more and so do not deserve it.

The problem with this logic is that we did *not* start out equal. All people are not born with the same opportunities, the same resources, or the same gifts. We are all different. As disciples of Jesus we can live responsibly in such a world by being grateful for what we have and sharing with those who have need. Love calls us to determine what we've been given and how to use it in service to others.

ACT JUSTLY

Detachment frees us from wanting and needing things. An abundance mentality helps us realize that we can share our resources because we have enough. The question of when to share is answered by Jesus' commitment to justice.

In Matthew 5:25-26 Jesus warns us: "Make friends quickly with your accuser, while you are going with him to court, lest your accuser hand you over to the judge, and the judge to the guard, and you be put in prison; truly I say to you, you will never get out till you have paid the last penny." Here Jesus advises us to deal with our temporal affairs justly. These mundane matters of taxes and payment constitute training grounds where the exchanges are fairly simple to understand and achieve. By learning what we "ought" to do in such settings, we take the first step toward developing a commitment to justice. Justice at this level is transactional; we are expected to honor our contracts and commitments.

In the story about paying taxes to Caesar (Matt. 22:16-22; Mark 12:14-17; Luke 20:21-26) Jesus deals with what appears to be economic and civil justice. His adversaries try to ambush the Lord, as they did in the incident of the adulterous woman. At face value it appears to be a no-win situation for Jesus. If he says, "Yes, we should pay the taxes," many of his followers might have revolted; they detested Roman taxes. If Jesus answers, "No, we should not pay the tax," Jesus could be arrested for encouraging unlawful behavior.

Jesus breaks down the illusion of this false dilemma with his sage response. After asking for and inspecting the coin, he replies, "Then render to Caesar the things that are Caesar's, and to God the things that are God's" (Luke 20:25).

There is more here than economics and civil justice. Jesus shrewdly makes the point that the money is not God's; God has no use for it. The law requires the tax to be paid, and Jesus makes it clear that people are accountable to the law, even if they disagree with the law, as he knows many of his followers do. Extending this logic, we are led to understand that people are also accountable to God's law, whether they agree with it or not. In both cases, the requirements are not subjective. They are not binding solely on those who believe. The law exists for all. Every driver knows that if someone is pulled over for speeding, claiming not to know the speed limit is irrelevant. The driver is required to know and obey the law.

In this exchange Jesus answers the challenge about transactional justice—the question of paying taxes—with a response that calls people to transformational justice. He deftly conveys to his followers—and especially to his accusers to whom his remarks are directed—that whether or not one believes in Jesus and his Father, God's law is still binding. People are accountable for rendering to God the things that are God's: love, mercy, and compassion.

Dealing with our wealth presents a complex challenge.

Richard Rohr founded and directs the Center for Action and Contemplation in Albuquerque, New Mexico, and has written several books on spirituality. In the early 1990s I had the opportunity to hear Father Rohr speak. He began his remarks by pointing out that if we read the Gospels carefully, we see they are not so much about love as they are about justice. Jesus' justice means much more than justice in financial or civil matters. The justice of the Gospels encompasses all facets of our lives. In all things we are called to act justly.

Developing a spiritually mature understanding of justice requires us to bring this virtue to bear on challenges that go beyond economic issues. We are called to act justly not only in our own affairs but to treat others justly and to defend justice. It requires us to honor our moral and spiritual commitments and covenants. What about justice for the underrepresented, like the homeless or the illegal immigrants working in our fields?

Jesus' question in Luke 12:57, "Why do you not judge for your-selves what is right?" is rhetorical. We are able to judge. We know when we've made commitments or received services for which payment is due. In the same way we know when we should help. We know when peo-ple are suffering and need compassion. Jesus calls us to act justly, from the simplest monetary debt to the very highest demands of spiritual responsibility in defending justice. We must all render unto God the things that are God's.

From Virtue to Practice

As Christians living in a modern age, dealing with our wealth presents a complex challenge. We experience tremendous pressure to accumu-late, to own, and to buy happiness. How do we act on these concepts of detachment, abundance mentality, and justice in our daily lives? How much is okay to earn? How much should we give? Should we give to individuals or to organizations? Which ones? These are among the hard-est questions of Christian discipleship, and there are no simple answers.

Kahlil Gibran (1883–1931), a Lebanese-American artist and poet, was born in the Christian Maronite town of Bsharri in what is now northern Lebanon. He came to the United States with his mother and sisters in 1895. His spiritual writings deal extensively with Christianity. In his most famous work, *The Prophet*, he wrote:

> It is in exchanging the gifts of the earth that you shall find abun-dance and be satisfied.
>
> Yet unless the exchange be in love and kindly justice, it will but lead some to greed and others to hunger. . . . And before you leave the market place, see that no one has gone his way with empty hands.
>
> For the master spirit of the earth shall not sleep peacefully upon the wind till the needs of the least of you are satisfied.[5]

As disciples of Christ we must prepare ourselves for compassionate generosity. Our ability to give charitably is founded on two basic quali-ties: (1) a willingness to give, and (2) a capacity for giving.

Willingness to Give

In the mid-1980s I was in college and volunteering with a church youth program to conduct retreats for high school students. About a dozen of us were finishing up a planning session one cold December night. As we stepped into the parking lot behind the offices, I could see my breath in the cold air. Each of us was bundled warmly in thick jackets, scarves, and gloves to ward off the chill.

As we stood debating in the parking lot about whether there was some place still open that might serve coffee and dessert, a man well beyond middle age approached us. He was dressed less protectively in loose-fitting, light clothes intended for a different season. His neck and head were bare. Despite the obvious cold, he whistled a happy tune. As he neared, our conversation fell off. When he was perhaps ten feet away, he regarded us and, in a very pleasant voice, said, "Pardon me, do you have any spare change for food?"

Our answers came quickly, "No." "I'm sorry, no." "Nope."

He nodded, smiled, and gave us his blessing: "Have a nice evening." He resumed his whistling and walked back toward the alley. Stopping at the dumpster, the man opened the lid and began to rummage through the garbage. How long this scene lasted—ten seconds or ten minutes—I really don't know. It was timeless. Not one of us moved. We were frozen but not by the cold. Soon the man found a half-eaten sandwich and began to eat it as he walked away. Not one of us standing there commented on what we'd just seen and done. Not one of us went out for dessert.

All these years later I am still embarrassed when I recall this moment. As I reflect now on the things Jesus said and did, try as I might, I cannot find a single instance in the Gospels where Jesus said anything akin to, "Feed the hungry, unless you think they're losers, lazy, or will use it to buy booze." Jesus gave us no criteria for judging when not to give. He only called us to be generous. There are two simple ways to express our willingness to give.

First, give in the moment. When the hungry ask, give. Do what is in your power to do. Don't worry about their motive. If they really do need it, then you have been generous. If it's a scam, then they have lied and you have still been generous. If you don't like to give cash, carry gift certificates for fast-food restaurants in your area. Or keep a supply of dry nonperishable foods in the car (fruit leathers are a good one). Find a way that's comfortable for you to give.

Second, support organizations that work for change. Compassion is not limited to spontaneously giving to the hungry when they ask. Compassion also includes supporting efforts to improve the conditions that lead to social injustices like poverty and hunger. Organizations that lobby for social reforms, offer job training and life skills, and assist individuals and communities increase their capacity to be self-sufficient need our support. These organizations address social challenges systemically, and supporting them is no less compassionate.

Capacity for Giving

The second step in our preparation for charitable giving is to live beneath our means, because we cannot give what we do not have. We increase our capacity for giving by consuming less, a difficult goal in our instant-gratification society.

Credit cards encourage living beyond our means. Few of us treat credit cards as the emergency resources they ought to be. Instead we use them to purchase now what we cannot afford until later, if at all. Ironically much of it soon goes to the waste pile. Or worse, it goes into the garage or the basement.

Go for a walk around your neighborhood some Saturday in spring. Look at what is being stored in the garages on your block. I had a neighbor whose garage was so full that every time he opened the big door intended for vehicles, his possessions spilled out onto the driveway. The garage literally overflowed with the acquisition of years. Whenever he cleaned the garage, he would pull approximately half his belongings onto his driveway and front lawn. He would reorganize it, stack the boxes more neatly, pack things more compactly, and eventually put most of it back. The next time he opened the door, about the same amount of stuff would spill out onto the driveway. That scenario repeated itself several times over the four years we shared a fence.

> In the last century, a tourist from the States visited the famous Polish rabbi Hafez Hayyim.
>
> He was astonished to see that the rabbi's home was only a simple room filled with books. The only furniture was a table and a bench.
>
> "Rabbi, where is your furniture?" asked the tourist.
>
> "Where is yours?" replied Hafez.
>
> "Mine? But I am only a visitor here."
>
> "So am I," said the rabbi.[6]

Two strategies can help you increase your capacity for giving by living beneath your means. First, restrain your impulsivity. Don't purchase something the first time you see it. Before you buy it, consult one or more consumer advocacy sources to make sure your intended purchase is of good quality, good value, and safe. (In our house, any purchase over $150 requires a little online research.)

Next, dispose of your excess thoughtfully. Sell it through a garage sale or a consignment or second-hand store. Donate the proceeds to a worthy cause or use it as "need money" for those parking lot requests. The alternative is to donate your items (in good condition and working order—not garbage) to nonprofit organizations like the Salvation Army, the United Way, the American Red Cross, homes for single mothers, or shelters for runaway youth.

Love Is the Source

Detachment, an abundance mentality, and justice are the qualities that yield treasure in heaven. We express these by increasing both our willingness to give and our capacity for giving. However, if we perfectly accomplish these things but have not love, it means nothing. For example, we can increase our wealth through ruthlessness in our financial dealings, or we can give generously for self-serving purposes or false pretenses. The generosity we offer must be born of compassion and mercy. God wants us to develop not a history of charity but charitable souls. The amount or frequency of our giving is not the standard by which we'll be judged. God wants us to be vessels of mercy. God asks us to tap the wellspring of God's love residing within us—with the help of the Holy Spirit—and give to those in need.

Jesus told us we would always have the poor with us (John 12:8). He didn't eradicate poverty or heal all suffering. He could have taken care of these things, but he didn't. God did not send Jesus to solve all our problems; Jesus came to teach us how to live with our problems. This human life is difficult, full of hardships and disappointments interlaced with occasional joys and successes. Jesus' life and public ministry reveal how he responded to these problems: with compassion and charity.

From Jesus Priority to Essential Habit

**Practices for the 5th essential habit:
Build up treasure in heaven**
- *detach from earthly possessions*
- *maintain an abundance mentality*
- *act justly*

Reflect on the Gospel

Fear not, little flock, for it is your Father's good pleasure to give you the kingdom. Sell your possessions, and give alms; provide yourselves with purses that do not grow old, with a treasure in the heavens that does not fail, where no thief approaches and no moth destroys. For where your treasure is, there will your heart be also.—Luke 12:32-34 (see also Matthew 6:19-21)

Reflect on Your Priorities

What do you treasure? What do you need to let go of?
How does the way you earn, spend, or give your money reflect your faith?
What are the needs in your local community? What could you share?

Prayer

Abba, help me to treasure your love above all things. Teach me to understand how much I have to share. Grant me a generous heart and a charitable soul. Amen.

JESUS PRIORITY 6

~~~~~~

Seek God's Will

Gospel Story—*The Son of Man*

They did not understand that he spoke to them of the Father. So Jesus said, "When you have lifted up the Son of man, then you will know that I am he, and that I do nothing on my own authority but speak thus as the Father taught me. And he who sent me is with me; he has not left me alone, for I always do what is pleasing to him."

—John 8:27-29

This priority highlights Jesus' commitment to being of one mind with God. We find the Gospel evidence for his oneness with God in fourteen events recorded sixteen times, almost exclusively in John's Gospel. Although John is virtually silent regarding many of the other themes, he gives the most attention to the unity of Jesus and God the Father. Without John's Gospel, this concept would hardly surface as something Jesus consistently said; it is mentioned only once in Mark and just twice in Matthew and Luke. But it is suggested no less than nine times and explicitly stated two more times in John. Indeed, John's main theme is clarifying and proclaiming the nature and mystery of Jesus' relationship to God. Because it is so prevalent in John's Gospel, an accounting of what Jesus consistently said and did in the four Gospels would be lacking, even dishonest, if this concept were overlooked or ignored.

Most accounts that establish Jesus' oneness with the Father are similar to the story above. They imply a close, personal, even intimate relationship between Jesus and God. "If you knew me, you would know my Father" (John 18:19) and "he who rejects me, rejects him who sent me" (Luke 10:16) could be construed as affirmations that Jesus is a prophet. That is, he knows the will of God and speaks and acts on God's behalf. The two outstanding quotations, of course, are "before Abraham was, I am," in John 8:58 and "I and the Father are one," in John 10:30.

In all these passages, Jesus affirms his relationship, his oneness, with God. Jesus expresses this union with God in terms of his understanding and commitment to God's will. Jesus and God are one in mind. Recall the focus question: *What did Jesus consistently say and do during his public ministry that would be instructive?* He consistently defined his relationship with God primarily in terms of his complete dedication to God's will. We can aspire to this same habit of mind and spirit. We *can* be God-centered, aware of God's presence around us and especially within us. Consider the insights of a four-year-old girl about being one with God.

> I have, and have had for many years, a little plaything, a toy, something I like to consider and something which sparks off ideas in me. It is simply two circles of heavy copper wire linked together like two links of a chain. I play with this so often that at times I am quite unaware that I have it in my hands. On one occasion I was holding it so the circles stood at right angles to each other.
>
> Anna pointed to one of the circles and said, "I know what that is—that's me. And that's Mister God," she said, pointing to the other. "Mister God goes right through my middle and I go right through Mister God's middle."[1]

Four-year-old Anna expresses so simply a deep truth: God is in us. It is a paradox that we are so close to God, yet accessing God can be so difficult. It's hard enough to find God's will when life is good. When life is painful, it's easy to feel that God is impossible to find. For this reason, we must be especially careful in prayer during times of hardship. When we suffer, our normal human desire is to pray for the suffering to end. Remember that discerning God's will without regard for personal needs or hopes is precisely the example that Jesus gave us in the garden at Gethsemane. That strength of resolve was not new for Jesus; he'd spent his whole life constantly seeking God's will. His confidence in discerning God's will faithfully gave him the strength to go on. Jesus did not let the devastating circumstances of his passion influence his commitment to the will of God.

Like Jesus, we can cultivate the habit of seeking God's will—always. Life sometimes creates hurdles that make such a habit hard to maintain. We typically encounter five barriers to continually discerning God's will:

- imperfect knowledge
- lack of urgency
- daily distractions
- perceiving the search for God's will as one among many tasks
- fear of sacrifice

What can we learn from the way Jesus dealt with these barriers?

Know God Through Jesus

The first reason it's hard to know God's will is that our human perspective limits us. We just can't know the mind of our Creator. Only human arrogance would presume to know the thoughts of God. Our limited human mind and soul cannot cross the chasm between God's infinite wisdom and our imperfect knowledge and understanding; only God can. God made this crossing in Jesus. It should not be surprising that bridging this gap is impossible for us. Jesus told us that knowing the mind of God was reserved to him alone in Luke 10:22: "All things have been delivered to me by my Father; and no one knows who the Son is except the Father; or who the Father is except the Son and any one to whom the Son chooses to reveal him."

Because Jesus had this unique relationship with God, a constant focus on the teachings and actions of Jesus is essential to spiritual growth. Jesus came so that we could know God through him. He is "the way, and the truth, and the life" (John 14:6). Recall the first chapter of John: "To all who received him, who believed in his name, he gave power to become children of God" (John 1:12). To be children of God requires only that we commit ourselves to God's will and make our actions and words consistent with God's desire to bring mercy and charity to others *through us.* Jesus is our model for uniting our will to God's will. This is the value of the WWJD question *What would Jesus do?* The question asks us to predict how Jesus would respond in a situation. It's implied that we answer the question by considering how Jesus responded to similar circumstances. We are probing the question *What* did *Jesus do?* Our central question is: *During his public ministry recorded in the Gospels, what did Jesus do most of the time?* The commitment to being "one with God" provides a fundamental answer. Jesus did only what was completely consistent with the will of God.

> *The greatest gift you can ever give those you love is to be always in a state of grace.*

Maintain a Sense of Urgency

Another reason we find it hard to keep God's will at the core of life is the illusion of time. We tend to think we have plenty of it, and so we have no sense of urgency regarding God's will. We are content to work God's will into our schedule as time allows because we believe that time is an abundant commodity. In fact, we don't know how much time we have.

Jesus tells parables to encourage his disciples to be prepared. The parables of the rich fool (Luke 12:15-21) and the wise and foolish maidens (Matt. 25:1-13), for instance, give clear instructions to his followers. "You also must be ready; for the Son of man is coming at an unexpected hour" (Luke 12:40; compare Mark 13:34; Matt. 25:13).

The first apostles lived out of this sense of urgency, filled with fiery passion for the kingdom. Believing that their day of salvation was imminent, they were completely dedicated to the mission of the gospel of Jesus. The question for individual spiritual growth is: *When will he come for you?* We have to be prepared for our personal meeting with Jesus. That's difficult because we don't know when that meeting will take place. It could be tomorrow or next week. It could happen next year or not for decades.

About ten years ago, just one week before my marriage, I asked my father for any advice he could offer on married life. He shared the wisdom he'd received under similar circumstances some thirty-seven years earlier from an old family friend and priest. It was brief, practical, and affected me in a profound way: "The greatest gift you can ever give those you love is to be always in a state of grace." His words are still working their magic on me, still shaping my life. Aspiring to be always in a state of grace characterizes the pro-active Christian par excellence. Striving for a state of constant grace implies the desire that your soul is always prepared. Being spiritually prepared in this way actively demonstrates our concern for God's will as critical to us, even urgent.

FOCUS DAILY ON GOD'S WILL

We are not in the habit of reflecting on God's will in the context of our daily lives. As a result, we think about it only occasionally—in church on Sundays, for example. It would be more valuable and instructive to ask ourselves, *What is God's will for me right now, when this homeless person is asking for help?* or, *What is God's will when I am starting an argument with my spouse?*

Mary, the sister of Lazarus, demonstrated this kind of focus. When Jesus enters the house of Mary and Martha, the latter gets upset when she finds herself doing all the preparations for their guest, while her sister, Mary, sits at Jesus' feet. When Martha complains, the Lord answers her, "Martha, Martha, you are anxious and troubled about many things; one thing is needful. Mary has chosen the good portion, which shall not be taken away from her" (Luke 10:38-42). Jesus praises Mary's preference for listening to Jesus rather than busying herself with the social obligations of hospitality.

It's very easy in our society to assume the role of Martha and quickly distract ourselves from the essential tasks of Christian discipleship. Living from day to day requires us to perform an unending series of repetitive tasks: cook a meal, do the dishes, fold the laundry, clean the house, and so forth. As much as we might like to pray and read the Gospels, someone has to prepare the next meal! Martha was trying to be a good host. By challenging her, Jesus tells Martha that while some hospitality is appropriate, Martha has allowed her concern for hospitality to take precedence over spending time with Jesus. Martha has denied herself the "good portion," his holy and healing presence.

Mary kept her focus on what matters most by placing herself at the feet of the Lord, wanting to be near him. Like Mary, we can focus our lives on God and place ourselves at the feet of the Lord. This means more than taking time out from all the busyness of life to reflect on the Lord. As we go about daily tasks we are to keep ourselves mindful of Jesus' teachings. All that we do will become an expression, however simple, of our desire to be near him.

SEE EVERYTHING AS A TASK OF LOVE

A fourth challenge when it comes to focusing on God's will is our inclination to plan when and how we will act on God's will: "I work at the soup kitchen on Thursdays" or "I go to church every Sunday." We see God's will as something we fit in between washing the laundry and grocery shopping. We create the illusion that doing the will of God is separate from the other tasks of life, but this is not so.

Doing the will of God is not just one more chore among the many tasks of life. It is *the* task of life. This does not mean we should not calendar our prayer or community service, but it does mean we need to be sure our commitment to God's will doesn't end there. These activities are only the beginning. The goal is bigger: to live so that we are constantly discerning and responding to God's will.

There is one task only: the task of love. We are called by God to live this life with love for everyone. All that we do can be an expression of God's love. However mundane the task, perform it with a generous spirit and grateful heart. The most insignificant task performed with love is tribute to God, and every act of charity or service done for self-gain or with hate—or worse, indifference—is a hollow offering to God.

ACCEPT SACRIFICE AS GAIN

Many of us struggle with discerning God's will because it conflicts with our own. What God and Jesus want us to be doing is hard work; it may not be "fun" in the traditional sense of that word. We are called to love, and love requires effort. We are called to put others before ourselves. Love means delaying personal short-term gratification.

This sounds like a sacrifice, and the word *sacrifice* carries a negative connotation. *Sacrifice* sounds like a loss, but it's not. I once heard *sacrifice* defined as "giving up something of great value for something of lesser value." This made no sense to me at all. This kind of "sacrifice" would be simply a foolish mistake. Does the merchant who found the pearl of great price regret selling everything he owned to obtain the pearl? No! He makes the trade specifically because the pearl holds greater value for him. He wants it more than anything else.

A real sacrifice involves giving up something of good value in order to obtain something else of greater value. Think of the baseball term *sacrifice fly*. The team sacrifices the player on first in hopes of scoring the run at home. Baseball players stay focused on the long-term goal: scoring runs. Sports concepts like this often offer powerful and valuable imagery for Christians. How do we score a run for God?

Christians in the game of life have the long-term goal of returning to God's love. Like the merchant, we make the trade of sacrificing short-term goals for long-term goals willingly because we have clearly established what we value. We know what is precious to us. Short-term goals almost always focus on material goals and earthly rewards. These short-term payoffs cannot compare to God's love!

To act on God's will, we learn to make sacrifices. We can let go of what we want right now for what we know we want for all eternity. We stop chasing material possessions and comforts when they conflict with God's will. A constant focus on and submission to God's will seems daunting because it hinges on self-denial: constantly putting God's will before our own. That's what Jesus did. It's not easy, but with the help of the Holy Spirit, we can do it too.

From Jesus Priority to Essential Habit

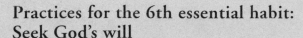

> ### Practices for the 6th essential habit: Seek God's will
>
> ♫ *know God through Jesus*
> ♫ *maintain a sense of urgency*
> ♫ *focus daily on God's will*
> ♫ *see everything as a task of love*
> ♫ *accept sacrifice as gain*

Reflect on the Gospel

I and the Father are one.—John 10:30

Reflect on Your Priorities

In what areas of life do you find your will in conflict with your understanding of God's will?

Is God's will an urgent concern for you? If not, what does feel "urgent" to you and why do think it claims your energy?

What part of yourself do you think you need to sacrifice? How could you seek God's guidance in letting go of whatever hinders living out God's will?

Prayer

Abba, bring me closer to you. Help me follow the example of your Son, to make your will the center of my life and a daily concern. Teach me that this life is a task of love. Grant me the wisdom and strength to see your love as the pearl for which all sacrifice is worthwhile. Amen.

JESUS PRIORITY 7

Accept Children as Precious

GOSPEL STORY—*Jesus and the Children*

The children were brought to him that he might lay his hands on them and pray. The disciples rebuked the people; but Jesus said, "Let the children come to me, and do not hinder them, for to such belongs the kingdom of heaven." And he laid his hands upon them.

—MATTHEW 19:13-15 (SEE ALSO MARK 10:13-16; LUKE 18:15-17)

JESUS' WORDS AND ACTIONS demonstrated that he saw children as precious. The Gospels of Matthew, Mark, and Luke consistently portray his relationship with children as positive and protective, which was progressive for the culture. In a land and time in which children had few rights, Jesus proclaimed that they would "inherit the kingdom." Jesus showed us that the innocence of children was not something to be tolerated but something to which we should aspire by protecting, welcoming, and being like children.

PROTECT CHILDREN

Jesus said, "It is not the will of my Father who is in heaven that one of these little ones should perish" (Matt. 18:14). Children need our protection, and that protection begins at the physical level. They need to be fed, clothed, cared for, and supervised. They need to be protected from

97

those who would harm them. The media and the prisons are full of people who inflict harm on our children. A recent public service announcement reports that sexual predators solicit one out of five children over the Internet. We must be vigilant in guarding against these evils.

We hear that it takes a village to raise a child. This statement is true to an extent, but it doesn't tell the whole story. A loving parent or two can raise a child; they make the protection of their own child their constant concern. It does, however, take a village to raise *all* our children. An entire adult community must work collectively to protect the community of children. If we perceive any child to be in danger, we are required by Christian conscience to help. Christ calls us to protect all children. Most parents understand this obligation and offer immediate assistance when they perceive the need.

Some time ago, I took my children to a local play park designed for preschool-age children. My son walked up to the top of the rabbit hole slide, which cuts through a small hill, while I waited for him at the bottom. The slide entrance at the top is not visible from the bottom, so I was not aware that he had decided not to go down the slide but to go down the back staircase and head off in a new direction. A dozen children were going down the slide, so it took a few minutes before I realized he was no longer near. When it dawned on me that he was taking too long to slide down, I called to him loudly, and he did not answer. I ran to the top of the hill but could not see him. My wife and I began shouting his name. Almost immediately dozens of parents joined us. They asked what he looked like and what he was wearing. Within seconds a dozen or more parents were calling his name. With this troop of parents, he was found quickly. I was amazed at the involvement of these parents, who demonstrated perfectly the concept of "it takes a village." Jesus challenges us to practice this common concern for the welfare of all children.

Secular culture promotes ideas that place children's souls at risk.

The protection of children that Jesus asks of us, though, requires much more than their physical protection: "Whoever causes one of these little ones who believe in me to sin, it would be better for him if a great millstone were hung round his neck and he were thrown into the sea" (Mark 9:42; see also Matt. 18:6; Luke 17:2). Jesus is concerned for their spirit, their soul. We must expand the concern of the village to the spiritual safety of all children.

How are our children threatened spiritually? The secular culture promotes ideas that place children's souls at risk by making beliefs and activities in conflict with Christian living appealing and attractive. Below are five fundamental mind-sets that our profit-seeking economy sells hard to our young people. There are others, but these five attitudes are so pervasive that children can be overwhelmed and deceived by their destructive message.

1. Happiness comes from acquisition.
2. Physical/sexual attraction is the best way to start a relationship.
3. Desire alone is justification for any pursuit. (I want it, and therefore I am entitled to it and will get it.)
4. Being cool requires youth to separate themselves from family—especially from parents.
5. Violence is a legitimate strategy for pursuing personal desire.

Parents can take three actions to counter these powerful negative forces. First, make God and Jesus the center of family culture. Through daily family prayer and other faith-based activities, make *God* and *Jesus* everyday household words. Parents should also be mindful of the power of symbolism. How many examples of faith and belief can you find around your house? What do family members see when they spend time in the kitchen, the living room, their bedroom? I went on a scavenger hunt in our own home recently to look for proof that God is a part of our lives. I found ten crosses, four paintings or pictures, one tapestry, four statues, and two candles. There are five additional faith references, including our personal marriage prayer.

Our house is by no means a shrine. The tapestry is a simple Christmas theme with candles and poinsettias around sheet music for Handel's "Messiah." We like it so much we haven't taken it down. Many of the crosses are small; you might not notice them. Several are ceramic, including two the kids designed themselves. We also have a beautiful plate with a picture of a small church (thanks, Martha), a statue of the holy family carved from the ash of Mount St. Helen's (thanks, Cheryl) and a sketch of Mary holding the infant Jesus with the caption "and the light was for all time, and the Love was for all men" (thanks, Pat).

Our children know that some of these items were gifts and some were purchased. Some we made ourselves, and one is a family keepsake. We treat them all as precious, and the children know they are important. We incorporate them into our family prayer, often at their request. I believe that this has been one of the greatest positive influences on my children. They live in a home with an ample supply of rich symbolism. God is never far away.

Second, parents need to be vigilant about the media to which children are exposed. Be careful about which movies they see, what music they listen to, and what books and magazines they read. Be compulsive about monitoring their access to the Internet. Put the family computer in a common area—the family room. Unsupervised access to the Internet is a bad idea. Even by accident, children and teens can be exposed to deeply disturbing images.

Of course, television continues to do some of the greatest harm. Anyone who has watched a child under the age of six stare numbly at the barrage of Saturday-morning commercials knows the power that the media hold over young minds. Study after study has validated this fact: children are impacted by the images they see on television. Long after the television is turned off, the images continue to replay themselves on a child's internal image screen. Research has demonstrated the relationship between television viewing and behavior. When we watch too much of the wrong kind of images, they change us. We become desensitized to violence, lust, profanity, and more. While some still argue that the research is inconclusive, the American Psychiatric Association has declared "the debate is over." Be selective and judicious about the media to which your family is exposed.

Finally, if you are a parent, talk with—not to—your children every day. Communicating effectively with your children is essential, because you cannot protect them if you do not know their struggles. That requires listening. Start this habit as early as possible, and it's never too late to start. This third goal of listening to and talking with children is critical.

In the late 1990s I was working at a K–8 school in California. I invited a facilitator to conduct a workshop on communication for parents and their junior high students. The evening provided parents with one of the best methods I have found for helping parents listen and talk to children. To get both groups to really listen to one another, the presenter encouraged them to try what he called "the appointment." Whenever a child needs to talk to a parent or a parent to a child, either can ask for an appointment. The rules for the appointment are:

1. Whoever asks for the appointment can say anything he or she wants. The person should focus his or her comments on the four H's: What makes me happy? What gives me hope? What haunts me? What hurts me?
2. The other person listens without interruption or reaction.
3. When the speaker is finished, the listener says, "Thank you for telling me. I love you very much." The listener then hugs the speaker.
4. The appointment is over.
5. If the listener wants to respond, he or she must ask for another appointment. This follow-up appointment should be at least several hours after the initial appointment; a day is better.
6. The same rules apply to each appointment.

It is highly recommended that parents practice by being the first to ask for an appointment and delivering good news. Tell your child, for example, "I am so happy that your grades have improved!" Practice the skills of the appointment when the topic is pleasant and noncontentious, because the unpleasant will happen. That's part of life. Children will make poor choices at times; that's what children do. Parents are not expected to raise perfect children but to guide them patiently with understanding when they are not perfect. Parents have a better chance of effectively communicating with their children in difficult situations if they have practiced the skill of listening without interruption or reaction.

By practicing these three simple strategies of (1) making God and Jesus the center of your family culture; (2) being vigilant about the messages to which you expose yourself and your children; and (3) listening to your children every day, you can combat the anti-Christian media that bombard us on a daily basis. You can more fully achieve Jesus' directive: protect the children.

WELCOME CHILDREN

Jesus promised, "Whoever receives one such child in my name receives me" (Matt. 18:5; see also Mark 9:37; Luke 9:48). Welcoming a child is one of the simplest ways to follow the example of Christ. It takes only intention and a smile to welcome children, to put them at ease. Children more easily understand this truth than adults. When my children and I play in the park, we tend to have a lot of fun, running and laughing a great deal. Often we find other children watching us. These children rarely ask to join without an invitation. Both my children are very comfortable inviting others to join us, and the invitation is almost always accepted. I rejoice when my son or daughter approaches another child, a stranger, and extends an honest invitation in complete trust and innocence. "Do you want to play with me?" "Do you want to be my friend?" Sometimes these children will first look at me cautiously and raise their eyebrows as if to ask, "Is that okay? Can we play too?" My children answer for me. "C'mon, let's play!"

Children are inclusive by nature. At the park any child can join in the play as long as he or she will be nice. Children do not, by nature, discriminate. They do not exclude other children who differ from them in color, race, socioeconomic status, or even language. None of these is a barrier; anybody can play.

It is interesting, even humbling, that children achieve in a matter of minutes what has eluded adult society for hundreds of years. This is the real challenge of being childlike—to accept others as a habit. Children do so because they have had no training, no indoctrination that teaches them to behave any other way. Children are prewired for gentleness and love.

Consider the opportunities you have to welcome children. This could be as simple as offering a kind word at the supermarket. Give a smile and a wave to students at the school crossing near your home. Responding politely and patiently to a child's question at the local library makes a child feel welcome. How do you react when the neighbor kids come to your door raising funds for school? Every interaction with a child provides a chance to respond as Jesus did. Give the children your blessing.

Be Like Children

Jesus said, "Unless you turn and become like children, you will never enter the kingdom of heaven" (Matt. 18:3; see also Mark 10:15; Luke 18:17). A child's understanding of love is profoundly simple and powerful, and so they are especially close to God. While there are many more characteristics of children than can be treated here, the following three are universal. These can be found in every child, in every culture, in every nation on earth. Children offer perfect praise; they trust; and they are affectionate.

Perfect Praise

I was in the U.S. Virgin Islands at Christmastime in 1997. On Christmas Eve my wife and I attended a local church to enjoy the children's Christmas pageant. As an elementary school principal, I had witnessed some excellent student productions, and I was looking forward to seeing what these children had prepared.

The production was chaotic, without the usual organizing principles in force. The children did not know their lines; neither did they know where to stand or the sequence of events. They clearly had not sung together often or recently. Their costumes ranged from poorly thought-out to nonexistent. It was painful to watch, and I was embarrassed for them.

The parents were not embarrassed at all. They were jubilant; they were delighted. They knew the truth beyond the facts. They knew that it did not matter if the children had memorized their lines or if the costumes were poor. It did not matter that the singing was less than perfect or that the church was a frenetic mass of disorganized energy. The children were celebrating the birth of Christ—that made it beautiful. They were there in the church, praising God, completely secure in their desire to do so. It was just simple and sincere praise.

Learn to make connections to God spontaneously, like children.

More recently my wife and children were passing near my office as they drove home. My wife asked our then four-year-old, "Sarah, would you like to leave a note on Daddy's car?"

Sarah was enthusiastic. "Yeah!"

My wife pulled the car over and found a pen and some paper. "What should we say in our note to Daddy?"

Sarah responded immediately. With perfect clarity she instructed my wife thus: "Let's say, 'Glory to God in the Highest.'" After recovering from mild shock, my wife agreed that this was a good message, and so the note was written and left on my windshield.

How is it that this would occur to a four-year-old and not the adult in the car? And how is it that the adult should be surprised? Children offer up perfect praise because they are not self-conscious. They don't worry about what others will think of their thoughts or words. Children are pure of heart. In the silence of their soul there is no evil intent, no malice of forethought. They do not know skepticism but instead assume the best. They are honest and unpretentious. Their praise is simple and spontaneous.

Each morning before I go to work, my wife gives me a blessing. It's brief and spontaneous—she says what is in her heart. I also give her a blessing. We've been doing this for perhaps a year. Both our children now accept the invitation each morning to lay their hands upon my head and give me a blessing. Their prayer is simple and sincere. I know it is heard: "God bless you forever and all, Daddy."

Learn to make connections to God spontaneously, like children. Praise God for the sunrise, the new day, those who prepared your food, and those who serve. Make your praise simple. Sing, shout for joy, and clap!

Trust

Children develop trust because they must; they are completely dependent on their parents for all that they need. As children grow up, especially in the United States, a nation that holds success and self-sufficiency in the very highest regard, it is difficult to truly trust God.

Once as I sat in a hospital waiting room I observed three small children in the room, unattended. I watched them, smiling at some of their comments and antics. They must have noticed, because after a while the youngest, a girl of perhaps five years of age, came and spoke to me. Within minutes she had crawled up onto my lap. I told her that it was probably not a good idea for her to be so affectionate with a stranger. She giggled and told me with her laugh still fading, "You're not a stranger." This trust of adults is built-in. Children unlearn it only through training that adults provide. As we grow, life's pain, disappointment, and occasional meanness can weaken our willingness to trust. We transmit this attitude of mistrust, often unintentionally, to children.

On November 12, 2001, moments after leaving Kennedy International Airport, a plane fell out of the sky and landed in Queens, New York. More than 260 people were killed. In an interview, an area resident said, "Man! If that plane had come down one block earlier, I'd have been killed. I guess God was looking out for me." And the unspoken extension of that belief would be that God must *not* have been looking out for those that lost their lives.

Sentiments like this confuse our notions of trust in God, as would any personal tragedy or loss. But they also raise the question of what it really means to trust God. It does not mean we will be protected or get what we wish for; we all know that doesn't always happen. But neither does it happen for children. We don't give them everything they want. Good parents try to give not what *children* think they need but what *the parents* think children need.

Adults often fall into the misguided notion that we actually know what we need. But God sees what we cannot see. To trust God does not mean we trust that God will give us what *we* want but that we will get what he knows we need, or that, through us, others will get what they need.

As you go about your day, remember that we are not in control of life. We can control only one thing: how we respond to life. Take responsibility for responding in a manner that would please God, and trust that all else is in God's hands. If God wants you to accomplish something, trust that it will be accomplished.

Affection

Recently my wife was quizzing our children on the concept of opposites. When she said, "hot," they answered, "cold."

"Up," she continued.

They yelled back, "Down!"

"Pushing."

Without hesitation our daughter shouted, "Hugging!" Her affectionate frame of mind and gentle spirit interpreted *pushing* as an attack and came up with the best opposite—an embrace.

When I came home this evening, after working later than usual, my four-year-old son greeted me by smiling and yelling, "Daddy!" He ran to me, threw his arms around me, buried his face in my neck, and squeezed. After about thirty seconds of father-son bonding, he looked up at me and said, "Daddy, I am *so* glad you're home." How could I not smile?

The power of an affectionate child is compelling. Children give their affection freely, without expecting any reward. Their love comes with no strings. Their offer to hug or hold hands is hard to resist—and even harder to emulate. Here we see one of the attractions as well as one of the problems with childlike affection. It has a strong physicality about it: the touching, the hugging, the holding hands, the kiss on the cheek, and the deep embrace. If we are to become like children, then how shall we be affectionate toward God? It's hard to wrap our arms around God.

First, remember that Jesus encouraged us to be affectionate toward God in prayer. He invited us to use the name for God that he used: *Abba.* Consider finding a term of endearment to use in your conversations with God. My own model for this affection is my son, especially when he wants something from me. He comes into the room with a soft, almost hesitant voice and begins his request with a quiet, "Dad?"

Second, as an extension of our affection for God, be affectionate with people. If this is difficult, start with the best practitioners of affection: children! They ask so little and give so much. They give hugs for free, almost always on request, and often unsolicited. Spending time with children will help you stay connected to that honest affection, and it will increase your capacity to be like them.

From Jesus Priority to Essential Habit

> ### Practices for the 7th essential habit: Accept children as precious
> *🙠 protect children*
> *🙠 welcome children*
> *🙠 be like children*

Reflect on the Gospel

See that you do not despise one of these little ones; for I tell you that in heaven their angels always behold the face of my Father who is in heaven.
—Matthew 18:10

Reflect on Your Priorities

What children do you know who need protection? How can you contribute to their spiritual safety?

What are some easy ways you could make the children in your life feel welcomed?

Think about your ability to be affectionate with others, especially with children, and compare this to your frame of mind in prayer. How can you be more affectionate with people and with God?

Prayer

Abba, help me to protect all your children. Teach me how to welcome them as your Son did. Grant me the wisdom to worship you with childlike affection, trust, and praise. Amen.

JESUS PRIORITY 8

Live with Humility

GOSPEL STORY—*Who Is the Greatest?*

They came to Capernaum; and when he was in the house he asked them, "What were you discussing on the way?" But they were silent; for on the way they had discussed with one another who was the greatest. And he sat down and called the twelve; and he said to them, "If any one would be first, he must be last of all and servant of all."

—MARK 9:33-35 (SEE ALSO LUKE 9:46-48)

IN THIS STORY and similar ones, Jesus instructs his disciples in the importance of humility. Jesus often told his listeners that "the last will be first." Through his parables and his reaction to events around him, Jesus praises humility in a range of human situations including work, socializing, and prayer. In Matthew 5:5 Jesus proclaims, "Blessed are the meek, for they shall inherit the earth." He cautioned us to be humble before God, and humble with one another. His actions and teachings that reflect this principle contain three characteristics we can adopt: Rely on God's Mercy; Presume the Lowest Place; and Sacrifice Your Ego.

RELY ON GOD'S MERCY

Recall Jesus' parable of the tax collector (Luke 18:9-14) who raises his voice to God in prayer: "God, be merciful to me a sinner!" He can't even look up. He stands in the back beating his breast. And this man, Jesus tells us, is forgiven. Note that Jesus directed this story to those "who trusted in themselves that they were righteous." The tax collector demonstrates that it is trust in God's mercy, not in one's merit, that assures forgiveness.

We receive mercy when we earnestly desire to be good. We demonstrate that desire by trying even though we may not succeed. In sports, we tell young people, "It's not whether you win or lose, it's how you play the game." We love them no matter what, and we're proud when they give their personal best. When that best is far below everyone else's best, we don't punish them. We celebrate their achievement. Abba is a good, loving parent. God wants are our best and rejoices when we conquer a hurdle that's been difficult. God is also patient with us, knowing that not all our efforts will be successful. We can't always win, improve, or succeed. Although Jesus did encourage us to "be perfect" (Matt. 5:48), God knows that for us humans it's not very likely.

There is nothing you can do to earn your way into heaven. God is perfect, and when we return to God, we shall be perfected in God's love. That will not happen as a result of any act on our part, as if we could wake up one morning and say to the Almighty, "Okay. Now, I am good enough to be in your presence." The idea is absurd. Our reunion with God is assured by God's mercy, not by any state of holiness or grace that we can achieve on our own.

PRESUME THE LOWEST PLACE

Jesus teaches the virtue of humility again when, at dinner in the home of one of the Pharisees, he tells the parable of the wedding guest (Luke 14:7-11). He instructs: when you go to a wedding, go and sit at the lowest place. This marriage feast could be an allegory for our arrival at God's feast. When we approach the feast that awaits us, will we presume to run up to the head of the table and sit at God's right hand?

James and John, the sons of Zebedee, tried to do just that (Matt. 20:20-28). In an act that most of us would consider an embarrassing social mistake, their mother approaches Jesus with this request:

"Command that these two sons of mine may sit, one at your right hand and one at your left, in your kingdom." Jesus very politely tells them, "To sit at my right hand and at my left is not mine to grant, but it is for those for whom it has been prepared by my Father."

Jesus makes it clear that in heaven, as on earth, it is not the place of the guest to presume her or his station. The host extends the invitation. Honor is given, not earned. Recognition is a gift, not a right. The guest should presume the lowest station.

God wants our best and rejoices when we conquer a hurdle.

On several occasions Jesus teaches his followers to be last—servants of all. When the disciples are arguing among themselves about who is greatest, Jesus says, "Whoever would be great among you must be your servant, and whoever would be first among you must be your slave; even as the Son of man came not to be served but to serve" (Matt. 20:26-28).

On a similar occasion when Jesus knew his disciples had been talking on the road about which of them was greatest, he called them to him and said, "If any one would be first, he must be last of all and servant of all." He then took a child in his arms and said, "Whoever receives one such child in my name receives me" (Mark 35-37; see also Luke 9:48). Remember that children in the time of Jesus had little power or influence. By making a child equal to himself, Jesus taught his apostles that greatness is measured by the degree to which you place yourself at the service of those who have the fewest resources, the lowest standing, and the greatest need.

Brother Lawrence was assigned to work in the kitchen of his monastery. He dreaded the assignment, the only job that prevented a monk from participating in the religious exercises of the community. Preparing meals for the community consumed all his time, making it impossible to join in the prayers, which he cherished. He disciplined himself to devoting his tasks to God. He was reduced to peeling potatoes for the Lord. Brother Lawrence's experience reminds us that often we do not get to choose our tasks; sometimes these are determined for us. We may always choose our attitudes though. We can decide to perform our tasks, however small, with great love and humility.

SACRIFICE YOUR EGO

In describing her new album of traditional religious hymns, an accomplished songwriter recently said that the music was already good; she was "just trying to get out of its way." Similarly, we can apply this notion to our need for humility and admit that "God is already good, I just need to get out of God's way."

Jesus' commandment that we love one another requires a commitment from us to act for others. Whenever we prevent God's love from helping others, we are in God's way. Personal prayer and contemplation can reap tremendous benefit in getting us out of God's way by putting our ego into perspective. *Ego* defines that human tendency to preserve our own positive self-concept. It is the source of false pride and narcissism.

You cannot be focused on God's will or serve as a vessel of God's love if you are preoccupied with feeding your pride, elevating your standing, or improving your position. You use a great deal of energy sustaining the actions that improve how others perceive you. With so much energy devoted to yourself, little remains available for others. Jesus gave all his energy to others; he sacrificed his ego.

Perhaps one of the strongest examples of the need to let go of our ego is the parable of the laborers in the vineyard (Matt. 20:1-16). The workers who toiled only for the last hour of the day are given a full day's wages, more than they deserve or have legitimately earned. The laborers who worked all day resent this unfair distribution of wages.

The owner of the vineyard knows that these workers come late. He knows they likely did not work the day before. He knows also that if he only pays what was earned, these workers might go home without enough to feed their families. He pays them more than they have earned out of his compassionate understanding.

Rather than rejoice for their fellow workers, those who'd put in a full day feel cheated. They argue that they deserve more because they contributed more. The source of discontent for these workers is their insistence on comparing the other workers to themselves. They want the other workers to be paid using their own wages as the standard.

Jesus tried to lift his contemporaries out of their egocentric frame of mind and change their eye-for-an-eye brand of justice. He wanted God's children to stop saying, "What about me?" and start saying, "What about them? Are they okay?" The full-day laborers have to recognize that the vineyard owner's actions are just; both parties agreed to a full day's work for a full day's wages. That the vineyard owner chooses to be generous to others should be a cause for celebration, not complaint. The late workers got what they needed, given to them as a gift. That is an injustice to no one. The laborers in the vineyard aren't really objecting to the wages paid to those who worked for only the last hour. They object because they want to be paid proportionately more. It's about themselves—their ego. The story illustrates that being offended as the full-day laborers were is equivalent to a failing—an inability to rejoice in the good fortune of the other laborers or the generosity of the vineyard owner. Their ego prevents them from being humble.

Through the parable of the laborers in the vineyard Jesus reminds us that we are each called to work for the kingdom at different times and places. God does not punish those who come late but welcomes them. It doesn't matter when we show up in God's vineyard; a place is reserved for us at Jesus' table.

In his book *Mere Christianity*, C. S. Lewis, the renowned Christian author, wrote, "The real test of being in the presence of God is, that you either forget about yourself altogether or see yourself as a small, dirty object. It is better to forget about yourself altogether."[1] This is what Jesus did. He forgot himself altogether. He lived for others, responding to God's will by offering those around him healing, mercy, forgiveness, and charity. He achieved this through prayer that focused on God's will. Jesus detached himself completely from his own needs or desires.

Forgetting about one's self is a most difficult task because everywhere you turn—there you are! How do you begin to forget yourself? Earlier we explored the nature and value of sacrifice. The challenge of forgetting about your self is a kind of sacrifice.

Jesus did not worry about his reputation.

Our daily reflections could easily focus on this one issue of ego and never run out of material. Applying this notion of sacrifice helps us see that Jesus put all his energy into defending others instead of himself. Jesus did not worry about his reputation. He did not worry about winning, proving himself right, or being superior. He could have had all these things, but Jesus wasn't in it for himself. The greatest barriers to humility might be named in three simple words. Try removing three words from your vocabulary and see how it changes you: *I, me,* and *mine.*

Humility with Ability

As you practice Rely on God's Mercy, Presume the Lowest Place, and Sacrifice Your Ego, remember that this humility to which Jesus calls people must not be confused with weakness or false modesty. Jesus wasn't weak, and he was not afraid to demonstrate his abilities or authority. Humility does not mean you should pretend you do not have skills or cannot succeed. Indeed, God needs people with talent.

Do not doubt that you have this talent. Jesus said, "You are the light of the world" (Matt. 5:14). Who are we to argue with Jesus? One of the tasks of Christian discipleship, then, is for us to find our light, to find the gifts we've been given. Once found, we must learn how we can let our light shine for God's glory.

Why, though, does Jesus mention how silly it is to place a light under a bushel (Matt. 5:15)? He wants us to understand that this makes no sense. If the light is hidden, then its very purpose is lost. Once covered, the light no longer serves the only function it can serve. In the same way, when we fail to let our light shine, fail to let the gifts God gave us be a source of heaven's kindness and compassion, it is no longer possible to achieve the purpose for which we were created. We are meant to be, by design, heaven's light.

Trying to be as great as God wants us to be without ego, without presuming recognition or reward, is hard. We achieve this by remembering that each of us is made in God's image, just less than angels. Each human soul is no greater but also no less than any other in God's eyes. When we use our God-given greatness, we can take no credit for our achievements because they do not come from us but from God. When we allow God to work through us, the results are God's accomplishments. It is the spirit of God working in us that accomplishes God's will.

Understanding that God gets the credit saves us from the trap of seeking reward or recognition. Such accolades are not good for us; they tempt us to serve for payment in the form of praise from others. We become nice in order to be noticed. Jesus had something to say about this: "Whenever you give alms, do not sound a trumpet before you, as the hypocrites do in the synagogues and in the streets, so that they may be praised by others. Truly, I tell you, they have received their reward" (Matt. 6:2, NRSV). The danger is that pride can become the source of our motivation.

Humility means that we rejoice in having been called to the labor. We celebrate that we are invited to be vessels of God's mercy, grateful for the honor to serve.

From Jesus Priority to Essential Habit

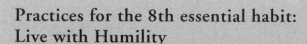

> ### Practices for the 8th essential habit: Live with Humility
> *⌇ rely on God's mercy*
> *⌇ presume the lowest place*
> *⌇ sacrifice your ego*

Reflect on the Gospel

Jesus called them to him and said, "You know that the rulers of the Gentiles lord it over them, and their great men exercise authority over them. It shall not be so among you; but whoever would be great among you must be your servant, and whoever would be first among you must be your slave; even as the Son of man came not to be served but to serve."—Matthew 20:25-28 (see also Mark 10:42-45)[2]

Reflect on Your Priorities

Do you trust in God's mercy, or are you trying to earn your way into heaven?
What recognition or reward is feeding you? Are your actions motivated by the return you might earn?
What part of your ego is in God's way? If you no longer worried about how others perceive you, what would you be free to do for God?

Prayer

Abba, your mercy is my salvation. Help me to be humble by presuming no reward or recognition and by keeping my focus on the needs of others. Amen.

Making the Jesus Priorities Our Essential Habits

OUR PERSONAL HABITS

In the preceding chapters we have explored what Jesus said and did most often during his public ministry, identifying these habits for our daily living. Our findings are not surprising perhaps. All of them can be contained, as Jesus said, in the Great Commandment. Love your neighbor as your expression of your love for God. Christian living is not a difficult concept, so why do we see so little evidence of it? I asked my daughter for her "children shall inherit the kingdom" wisdom on this matter. At age seven, Sarah understands that love is the core of the Christian message.

"Sarah, why is it so hard to be like Jesus?"

"It's not hard," she corrected me, as if I'd just told her adding one plus one was difficult.

"You just have to be nice," brother Nicholas added.

"Why is it so hard for some people to be nice?" I pursued.

"Because they don't have love in their heart," Sarah concluded.

In the initial overview, I touched on the fact that the eight priorities, like the Ten Commandments, can be divided into two groups: those about relationship with God and those about relationship with others. *Pray* and *Seek God's Will* focus on our relationship with God. These priorities lead to habits that help us explore the nature and depth of God's law of love. Seeking unity with God's will is both the first act and the final goal of every disciple of Jesus.

The priorities *Heal, Love, Spread the Word, Build Up Treasure in Heaven, Accept Children as Precious,* and *Live with Humility* reveal Jesus' hopes for how we would express that love. These priorities were not ends in themselves though. Jesus did not say and do them because he thought they would look good on a résumé or because he was just a really nice guy. His words and actions were his response to God's will. These visible manifestations of the love of God express Jesus' intention to act always in a manner pleasing to God. Our actions can also grow into habits that reveal our priorities—our desire and intent to be an agent of God's love. Remember, though, that we do not initiate this love. God initiates this love. Jesus calls us to join him by committing our lives to sharing God's love by serving others.

> *Jesus knew exactly what he was doing because he never forgot why he was doing it.*

I still remember my high school's motto: "A Man for Others." The complete mission statement fully develops the Jesuit philosophy, but these four words are powerful. At eighteen, I thought I understood the message: loving others is important. But "loving others" is more; those words express the core of Christian faith. That's why loving others is part of the Great Commandment: Love God, love others. Jesus was a man for others.

Each of Jesus' priorities points to the importance of placing the needs of others before our own interests. In the chapter about the priority to Heal we saw that Jesus never lost touch with his compassion for others. By responding in compassion, Jesus put others before himself, uniting his actions to God's will. In the chapter on Love we reflected on how Jesus responded to someone washing his feet. While dining as a guest in another person's home, he was not bothered by the interruption, by the woman's implied profession, or by the touch of her hands. He suffered his host to wait while a stranger wept at Jesus' feet and dried them with her hair. Jesus' concern for forgiveness was his motivation.

Jesus' priority *Spread the Word* teaches us to invite and share the mission with others—bringing them as guests to the banquet and into the fields as fellow laborers. For the priority *Build Up Treasure in Heaven*, we explored the challenges of increasing our willingness and capacity for responding charitably to those in need. The priority of Jesus concerning children encourages us to both welcome and protect the smallest members of our community. In the chapter about humility, we reflected on Jesus' call for us to be "last of all and servant of all" without recognition or reward.

Jesus' followers are asked to adopt this discipline, the mental and moral commitment to pursue God's will through our concern, compassion, forgiveness, and charity to others. Jesus' priorities serve as an effective spiritual tool, keeping us focused on this discipline. These eight essential habits are summarized on the following page with permission to copy the list for personal use. Consider placing it in a prominent place where you will see it often.

I began this journey to answer my own questions of faith. I wanted to know what message of comfort I could extract from the Gospel accounts of Jesus' life. I wanted to know: *What did Jesus consistently say and do during his public ministry that would be instructive for us?* As the priorities emerged, I realized that I could not understand fully *what* Jesus did until I explored *why* Jesus did what he did.

Integrating Jesus' priorities into our lives is not about merely imitating behavior. Behaviors flow from beliefs and principles. Significant changes in our spiritual health will be achieved when we make conscious changes in our spiritual commitments. When we ask why Jesus did what he did and reflect on Jesus' motivation, it can only lead us to one place: Christ's unceasing love for God and complete dedication to God's will. Jesus knew exactly what he was doing because he never forgot why he was doing it. Our own spiritual reflection and growth can begin with two questions: *What am I doing? Why am I doing it?*

Now let's look at these issues in the larger context of the faith community: *What are we doing? Why are we doing it that way?*

PRIORITY 1
Heal

- Stay deeply connected to compassion
- Say yes to strangers
- Do what is within your power to do
- See with the heart

PRIORITY 2
Love

- Show mercy no matter what
- Extend forgiveness without limit
- Love others as your expression of love for God

PRIORITY 3
Pray

- Pray alone
- Pray persistently
- Pray with others
- Pray simply

PRIORITY 4
Spread the Word

- Share the mission with others
- Invite everyone to God's banquet
- Challenge others and yourself to live the gospel

PRIORITY 5
Build Up Treasure in Heaven

- Detach yourself from possessions
- Maintain an abundance mentality
- Act justly in all things

PRIORITY 6
Seek God's Will

- Rely on the example of Jesus
- Maintain a sense of urgency by seeking to be in a state of grace
- Focus daily on God's will
- See all tasks as acts of love
- See sacrifice as gain

PRIORITY 7
Accept Children as Precious

- Protect children
- Welcome children
- Seek to be like children

PRIORITY 8
Live with Humility

- Rely on God's mercy—not your own merit
- Presume the lowest place
- Sacrifice your ego

HABITS OF THE FAITH COMMUNITY

At the close of the twentieth century, approximately 33 percent of the world's population professed to be Christian.[1] We don't know to what degree these billions are involved in the faith community, but conceivably millions consider themselves to be actively living out the faith. How could the priorities of Jesus' public ministry guide these communities of Christ's followers? My purpose is not to argue for or against any particular institutional church but to propose some characteristics of Christian communities consistent with Jesus' priorities. These may serve as unifying principles for the expression of the Christian faith.

Like Jesus' apostles, we too are destined for living in Christian community, compelled to come together because of our faith in Jesus. His commandment that we love our neighbor requires that we live in relationship with others. His advice for dealing with the sins of "your brother" (or "another member of the church," NRSV) presumes a faith community: "if you are not listened to, take one or two others along with you, that every word may be confirmed by the evidence of two or three witnesses. If he refuses to listen to them, tell it to the church." Jesus concludes with, "For where two or three are gathered in my name, there am I in the midst of them" (Matt. 18:16-17, 20), implying that we would gather in his name and that he wanted us to do so.

Jesus lived a life based on love, healing, prayer, compassion, charity, and humility. He called others to join him in this work, forming communities both among his chosen apostles as well as with the larger community of his disciples and followers. Our desire to remain faithful to what Jesus consistently said and did calls us to create communities that continue and extend the mission Jesus began.

Healing for All

In "Jesus Priority 1: Heal" we considered the importance of treating those around us with compassion and doing what is within our power to do. The first task for a group of Christian believers is to learn about the needs of the people and groups within and beyond the faith community. We need to answer the question *What do people really need?* We cannot have compassion for the suffering if we don't know anything about them. Is there anyone in need of shelter or food? Are there elderly who are lonely or need assistance? Are there adults who don't know how to read? Are there children who need protection? A Christian community works proactively to respond to needs in the local community among and beyond its membership.

What power does the community have? The Christian faithful can work with local government and private nonprofit organizations to determine what already is being done and what systems are already in place. When unaddressed needs are identified, the next question are *What is within our power to do? How can we contribute?*

In order to know what is within its power, a community of faith needs to know its members. When new people join a faith community, learning what gifts, skills, and experience they bring is vital. The leadership can meet with each family at least once a year to learn about them. (How is your family? Is there anything you need? What resources can you bring to the various ministries? How can we improve worship services for adults and children?) When the leadership really knows the members of the faith community, they can call upon them and invite them to help serve the needs of the local community. Personal invitation is the strategy Jesus used because it works well.

Any Christian community of faith must be strategic with its most valuable resource: the people of God. By developing a faith-organization that connects regularly with all its members, Christian communities can do what is within their power to be a source of healing—like Jesus.

Excluding No One

We have seen that Jesus said yes to strangers. The priority of welcoming newcomers extends beyond our individual practice of faith. The community of Christ's followers must work in concert to welcome strangers. This means more than posting someone at the door of the church to greet newcomers with a smile and a button. That's a good start, but it is not enough. We need to venture out to find the people who need to hear the good news and invite them to join us. That can become our ritual.

The Christian community hopes to extend Jesus' mercy and forgiveness. We accomplish this by excluding no one. This requirement should be the guiding principle in our liturgical worship.

The principle of excluding no one especially applies to children. Jesus wanted the children to be near him. Jesus did not send them away, and neither should we. Our worship needs to include and involve the little ones in our midst. When sermons are addressed to the young, not only do they gain, but mature members of the community also understand,

Personal invitation is the strategy Jesus used.

appreciate, and internalize the sermons better. The fundamental tenets of belief in God are not complicated: love God and love your neighbor. If we focus the gospel message to the needs of children, the whole community will be served. The greatest benefit of all would be that children look forward to Sundays: they will want to come. Like the children of Jesus' day, our children also wish to be close to Jesus. We should not hinder them.

An important consideration with regard to excluding no one is ritual. Jesus' concern for mercy and his attack on rules and rituals that threatened opportunities for mercy have obvious implications for Christian communities of faith. The problem with rules and rituals still exists today and in my experience hasn't changed much. Many worship services today have plenty of rules and rituals; paradoxically, they are ineffective at making people feel welcome—whether longtime community members or strangers. Our rituals need not separate us from others. Good ritual shows reverence for God and also encourages the participation of all who desire it. A prayer of the community designed in simple form allows newcomers to participate fully. Ritual can welcome friends and strangers, saints and sinners, to the table of the Lord.

Any community whose rituals or rules exclude others, that do not make them feel welcome, that punish them for not being perfect or a "member in good standing" is failing in its mission to extend the love that Jesus did. Jesus did not exclude; Jesus loved and challenged perfectly. He accepted sinners as they were and then challenged them to be more, to be better, to reach for holiness. We can do that too. In establishing norms for communal prayer or worship, let us give first consideration to Jesus' commitment to welcome all people.

Focusing the Money on the Mission

We have seen how securing treasure in heaven requires detachment. How do we apply the characteristic of detachment to an entire faith community? The community may need to detach from itself—to let go of its collective ego. Belonging to a faith community is not an end in itself. Jesus established a community of disciples with a mission. He did not spend three years meeting with the chosen twelve behind closed doors worshiping God and being nice to one another. Jesus' community aimed to usher in the kingdom of God: "to preach good news to the poor . . . to proclaim release to the captives and recovering sight to the blind, to set at liberty those who are oppressed" (Luke 4:18).

Consider the largest and most obvious attachment for most Christian communities—a church. The commitment to gather in a building the group owns carries with it a large price tag. A building is a tremendous investment; it costs money to build, maintain, decorate, clean, and protect. Naturally the community wants a place to worship. Gathering as a community strengthens the members and the group as a whole. Investing in a building may be worth it, but consider an alternative.

What if members gathered quarterly? What if they rented a space instead of owning it? What if all the money spent on fixed costs like utilities, maintenance, cleaning, and security were spent on hunger, shelter, and clothing for the poor? What if the money saved could be used to assist the unemployed or the working poor in the local community?

I am not suggesting that we tear down or sell our churches. The church building is just an example of the structures and programs sustained by the faith community members. The principle here is that a Christian community is called to direct a substantial portion (if not the majority) of its assets to its core mission: serving others. Christian communities need to take their pulse, regularly measuring how well they are achieving their mission.

Doctors Without Borders, established in 1971 by a group of French doctors, delivers "emergency aid to people affected by armed conflict, epidemics, natural or man-made disasters, or exclusion from health care." They carry out their mission "based solely on an independent assessment of people's needs, not on political, economic, or religious interests."[2]

How do potential donors know that the Doctors Without Borders stated mission is real? Let's look at how the organization's expenses in 2005 reflected their values. According to its Web site, 1.35 percent of donated funds were used for management and general expenses. That's less than two cents of every dollar. Another 12.94 percent was used for fund-raising, accounting for another thirteen cents. The remaining 85.71 percent was used for program services. For every dollar received, more than eighty-five cents went directly to providing medical services. Could the principle of allocating funds be applied in a local church?

When a community's efforts and assets become directed primarily inward—increasing its structures or infrastructures for the primary benefit of its members—it has lost sight of its purpose. As Christians we are not called by Christ first to gather in worship. We are called to serve others, to do what is within our power to do. We are called to love our enemies, to welcome the stranger, to protect the children, to heal the afflicted, to serve in humility wherever we find human suffering and need. The way we commit our community resources expresses our values. Our church annual finance report will reveal what percentage of our offerings are being spent on ourselves and what percent is being spent on what Christ asked us to do.

A community intent on continuing Jesus' mission directs its collective faith-work on charity and service where it's needed. It prioritizes its programs in relation to its mission, committing resources in response to the question *What do they need?* Programs and services critical to the core mission are funded first. Services that are important and support these critical functions are funded next. Those that would be "nice to have or do" are funded last.

Some years ago, I had the opportunity to attend a parish council meeting. The meeting's agenda included a question of whether to donate $250 to a local Christian food kitchen serving the poor a few blocks away. This particular parish had substantial assets, including a large church, K–8 school, preschool, and large gymnasium. The parishioners were mostly middle to upper middle class, and the parish budget easily exceeded one million dollars annually. No one criticized the service provided by the food kitchen; it was recognized as a well-run and valuable service. Nevertheless, the council spent forty-five minutes discussing the $250 donation, which represented about one fourth of one percent of the annual budget.

These are not bad people—they are generous and charitable. Why did such a decision consume so much time? They struggled over the donation because they did not have a shared understanding of the mission of their church. Without a clear mission, making decisions about programs, resources, and services becomes more difficult.

What standards can the Christian community adopt to ensure we are achieving the tasks Jesus gave us? The Christian faithful need a clearly defined mission and a commitment to dedicate a substantial portion of its financial and human resources toward achieving its core mission. A dedication to the things Jesus consistently said and did during his public ministry can guide that mission.

To measure their effectiveness, the faithful can solicit the judgment of the civic community, constantly asking, *To what extent is our presence and activity a benefit to the civic community?* Like a former well-known city mayor, we can walk around and inquire, *How are we doing?* The useful focus question is not *What happens among us?* but *What happens because of us?*

Finding Greatness in One Another

As we have seen, the humility modeled by Jesus does not require us to pretend we are less than other people. This humility requires us to acknowledge that each person is created in God's image, endowed by God with gifts, created by God in love, and so each person is worthy of our love. Christian humility asks that we find the talents in ourselves to serve those worthy of God's love.

Because God gave us each different talents, we can combine them in unique and powerful ways to respond to the need for love all around us. God through Christ is the beginning of synergy, in which the whole—the Christian community—exceeds the sum of its parts. When we act together we can accomplish so much more than the sum of what we could each achieve alone. The problems and needs all around us transcend our individual abilities and resources. We can transform ourselves into a gospel-centered, action-oriented people by banding together and drawing upon the gifts and talents each of us has to share.

> One day a rabbi, in a frenzy of religious passion, rushed in before the ark, fell to his knees, and started beating his breast, crying, "I'm nobody! I'm nobody!"
>
> The cantor of the synagogue, impressed by this example of spiritual humility, joined the rabbi on his knees. "I'm nobody! I'm nobody!"
>
> The "shamus" [custodian], watching from the corner, couldn't restrain himself, either. He joined the other two on his knees, calling out, "I'm nobody! I'm nobody!"
>
> At which point, the rabbi, nudging the cantor with his elbow, pointed at the custodian and said, "Look who thinks he's nobody!"[2]

This amusing story highlights the ludicrous goal of trying to outdo each other in humility. Jesus doesn't need us to be nobody, flogging ourselves with public confessions of inadequacy. He did not create us to be ordinary but extraordinary. Our goal is helping one another identify our extraordinary gifts in order to bring them to bear on local and global problems.

The Barriers: Why We Are Not Accomplishing More

Certainly across the globe Christian groups are doing a lot of good work. Unfortunately there is so much more to do, so many more people in need. How can we tap deeper into our collective resources? What prevents us from accomplishing more?

One of the primary means of interaction for a majority of Christians is attending Sunday services. It is critical for the community of faith to have time to together, but when these worship experiences are the predominant or the only center of activity for the faith community, they can become a barrier to achieving the goal of service. The task of Christian communities and of Christian individuals is the same: to be a source of forgiveness, healing, compassion, and charity. Recall Jesus' top three priorities from the introduction; Jesus models healing and loving three times as often as he models prayer. Remember Jesus quoting the prophet Isaiah: "This people honors me with their lips, but their heart is far from me." Prayer alone is not sufficient. Prayer without action is an incomplete response to the gospel of Jesus.

A community of Christian disciples can inspire and empower its members to do the loving work that Jesus called us to do, assisting individuals to act out their faith. Local churches continually face the challenge of taking the community beyond worship—mobilizing them to live the gospel. Any community founded upon Jesus encourages and empowers its members to serve the human community.

Systemic characteristics of organized religion tend to distance these goals from the ongoing life of the church. And typical organizational structures are not well suited to overcoming this barrier. Here we will briefly explore three common roadblocks to accomplishing more as Christians and some possibilities for working around them.

Inertia

The first challenge to greater achievement as servants of Christ is inertia—the tendency of any object (or person) to remain at rest until acted upon by an external force. When there are enough members in the club, it's easy to presume that "somebody else" will do what needs to be done. Crowd mentality allows us to be strong in vocal support and weak in sweat equity, because individuals in large communities are rarely asked directly to provide specific assistance or help. General appeals to the congregation during Sunday services will not yield great returns in volunteers. Jesus extended personal invitations because they work.

To overcome inertia, we could create small faith-in-action communities. These small teams of believers could respond effectively to specific community needs. Exactly how large should these teams be? Although "many hands make light work," too many hands make no work. Consider Jesus' team. He chose twelve men, none of whom had any previous training. Several did not know each other, and some probably did not even like each other at first. Each had different skills and gifts. At least four were fishermen; one was a scholar; and one was a tax collector. Jesus recruited them through personal invitation to the work of his Father. The disciples of Jesus did not become a team because of common language, common skin color, common age, common music styles, or even a common place of worship. The disciples became a team because they believed in a common mission; these twelve forever changed the world.

The disciples became a team because they believed in a common mission.

So if we too would forever change our world for the better, what size should we strive for in these small faith communities? The answer depends on the task, so a principle rather than a rule may be useful. Teams need to be large enough to share the task equitably and small enough to engage every member of the team actively and meaningfully.

Overwhelmed

A second barrier is the overwhelming nature of the work to be done. Considering a momentous task like feeding the hungry or providing shelter for people who are homeless can be psychologically paralyzing. These problems present enormous challenges. It's human to defend a lack of action by saying, "We'll never finish. We cannot even put a small dent in the hunger problem." The adage "A thousand-mile journey begins with one step" may help us take the first step, but how do we sustain the effort over time? It is difficult to start a task we know we will never finish.

Jesus started something knowing he would not finish, that he would be gone long before all the hungry had been fed and all the illnesses had been healed. Jesus got overwhelmed too. He was, at times, exhausted: "Foxes have holes and birds of the air have nests; but the Son of man has nowhere to lay his head" (Matt. 8:20; see also Luke 9:58). Jesus dealt with stress and fatigue by praying and getting away. But he was never gone for long, and he never stopped acting on his mission.

Jesus didn't solve all the problems, but he did make a difference. Like Jesus, we also cannot solve all the problems; we never will. We too, though, can make a difference, and that is what he calls us to do. Like Jesus, we need to be at peace knowing we will probably not finish what we started. Others will reap where we have sown. Jesus kept working, even though he knew his work would have to be finished by others. He started something and then trusted in the capacity of his disciples to continue his work after he was gone.

Jesus trusts us to do what he did—to start something, however humble. The important thing is not that we finish. The important thing is that we are engaged in the activity of serving others and that we work together to achieve more. We recruit new laborers to the field so that we can pass on the torch when we have finished our part of the labor.

Overstretched

The third factor that holds us back from accomplishing more in the name of Christ is the perception of many that they have already reached their limit of activity. They believe they are barely getting through each day. True, life today is more complicated than it was in the Holy Land two thousand years ago—and a lot more expensive. Many families have difficulty making ends meet. Not much time or money remains at the end of the month. However, people like to feel needed and useful. They may not stay in a faith community where they feel they cannot contribute meaningfully. At the same time, people can be scared away when asked to do more than they feel capable of doing. Churches need to be on guard against working volunteers to the point of burn-out. We can learn to pace ourselves as as we live in Christian community. The Christian life is not a sprint; it's a marathon.

We have a long way to go down the road of Christian fulfillment. In small faith communities, individuals can commit to whatever meaningful activity lies within their power to do. If we take the big objectives we need to accomplish and break them down into discreet tasks, we can share those tasks among the small faith community—asking each person to choose those tasks that they can carry out with their gifts and resources. If everyone contributes just a little, the effects would be almost miraculous.

The forces of inertia, of feeling overwhelmed, and of being overstretched are formidable. We can overcome these barriers by forming small faith communities, starting something, and allowing each member of the team to contribute to the labor according to his or her ability.

One People of God

Jesus' priorities offer a way to bridge differences among the many expressions of Christian faith. What would happen if all the disciples of Jesus united to accomplish the objectives set forth here? What if loving, healing, charity, and service became unifying forces in the ecumenical movement? Surely we can agree on these as the foundations for a life pleasing to Christ. What a powerful dream! We could bring together all Christian peoples to address areas of common need. If we are to be one people of God, united in Jesus' name, let our cornerstone be deep commitment to compassionate healing, merciful forgiving, charitable giving, and humble serving.

The Tree and Its Fruit

Throughout this book I have stressed that the teachings and works of Jesus are not for contemplation alone; they require action. Jesus said that "the tree is known by its fruit. . . . For out of the abundance of the heart the mouth speaks. The good person brings good things out of a good treasure, and the evil person brings evil things out of an evil treasure" (Matt. 12:33-35, NRSV; see also Matt. 3:8-10; 7:16-20; Luke 6:43-45).

Jesus showed us that our behaviors define us; he cares about our efforts. Christian discipleship is action, not position. Jesus seeks not confessions of faith but expressions of faith. These expressions spring from faith in Christ, and without the action this "faith" is false.

Christ was constantly on the move. He spent his days healing, forgiving, loving, and serving. He spent his nights in prayer, focusing on God's will. These are the works that are pleasing to God, that demonstrate real love for God. These are the actions that bear fruit. These are the actions Jesus modeled for us consistently during his public ministry. Living the priorities of Jesus will bring us closer to God.

GOSPEL CITATIONS FOR THE JESUS PRIORITIES

Heal

EVENT	MATTHEW	MARK	LUKE	JOHN
He Made Healing a Priority				
"Healing every disease and every infirmity"	4:23		6:18-19	
"Healed all who were sick"	8:16	1:32-34	4:40-41	
"Healing every disease"	9:35			
Healed them all	12:15			
Healed them all	15:30-31			
Healed them all	21:14			
"As many as touched it were made well."	14:35-36	6:55-56		
Man with an unclean spirit		1:23-26	4:33-35	
Casting out demons		1:39		
"He laid his hands ... healed them."		6:5		
"The power of the Lord was with him to heal."			5:17	
"In that hour he cured many of diseases."			7:21	
"some women who had been healed"			8:2	
"He ... cured those who had need of healing."			9:11	
"the signs which he did on those who were diseased"				6:2

Subtotal Events & Recordings: 15 Events   20 Times

He Said Yes to Strangers				
The Canaanite / Syrophoenician woman	15:22-28	7:25-30		
Healing a leper	8:2-3	1:40-42	5:12-13	
The centurion's servant	8:5-13		7:1-10	
The official's son				4:46-53
The Gadarenes (or Gerasenes) demons	8:28-32	5:1-20	8:26-39	
The hemorrhaging woman	9:20-22	5:25-34	8:43-48	
Jairus's daughter raised from the dead	9:18-19, 23-26	5:22-24, 35-43	8:41-42, 49-55	

Continued on following page

APPENDIX

Continued from previous page

EVENT	MATTHEW	MARK	LUKE	JOHN
Healing two blind men (Bartimaeus)	9:27-30; 20:29-34	10:46-52	18:35-43	
A dumb demonaic healed	9:32-33; also 12:22		11:14	
Healing a deaf man w/ a speech impediment		7:32-35		
Healing a blind man		8:22-25		9:1-7
An epileptic child is healed	17:14-18	9:14-29	9:38-42	
Healing ten lepers		17:12-19		

Subtotal Events & Recordings: 13 Events   29 Times

Demonstrated compassion

EVENT	MATTHEW	MARK	LUKE	JOHN
Healing a paralytic	9:2-7	2:2-12	5:18-25	
Simon Peter's mother-in-law	8:14-15	1:29-31	4:38-39	
The man with the withered hand	12:10-13	3:1-5	6:6-10	
Raising the widow's son from the dead			7:11-17	
Healing an infirm woman			13:11-13	
Healing a man with dropsy			14:2-4	
Healing a lame man on the sabbath				5:2-9
Raising Lazarus from the dead				11:1-44

Subtotal Events & Recordings: 8 Events   14 Times

Total: 36 Events   63 Times

Love

EVENT	MATTHEW	MARK	LUKE	JOHN
Mercy First				
"Blessed are the merciful."	5:7			
"Offer the other [cheek]."			6:29	
The good Samaritan			10:29-37	
"Be merciful"			6:36	
Eating with sinners	9:10-13			
Plucking the grain on the sabbath	12:1-8	2:23-28	6:1-5	
Not washing before meals			11:38-41	
Tradition of the elders	15:1-20	7:5-23		

Subtotal Events & Recordings: 8 Events   11 Times

Forgive without Limit

"First be reconciled to your brother or sister"	5:23-24			

Continued on following page

Continued from previous page

EVENT	MATTHEW	MARK	LUKE	JOHN
"If you forgive others, ... your heavenly Father will also forgive you."	6:14-15		6:37	
"Whatever you bind on earth shall be bound in heaven."	16:19			
"Whatever you bind on earth shall be bound in heaven."	18:18			
"I do not say to you seven times, but seventy times seven."	18:21-22			
The unforgiving servant	18:23-35			
"Whenever you stand praying, forgive."		11:25		
"If he repents, ... you must forgive him,"			17:3-4	
The adulterous woman				8:3-11
Washing the feet of Jesus	26:6-13	14:3-9	7:36-50	12:1-8
The prodigal son			15:11-32	

Subtotal Events & Recordings: 11 Events   15 Times

Love Others as God Loves

EVENT	MATTHEW	MARK	LUKE	JOHN
"[The Lord] has anointed me to preach good news to the poor."			4:18-19	
"Love your enemies. ... be children of your Father in heaven. ... Be perfect."	5:44-48		6:27, 35	
"...the great and first commandment. And a second is like it."	22:35-40	12:28-34	10:25-28	
"In everything do to others as you would have" them do to you."	7:12		6:31	
The great judgment	25:31-46			

Subtotal Events & Recordings: 5 Events   9 Times

Total: 24 Events   35 Times

Pray

EVENT	MATTHEW	MARK	LUKE	JOHN

Jesus Found a Quiet Place and/or Prayed Alone

EVENT	MATTHEW	MARK	LUKE	JOHN
"He rose and went out to a lonely place, and there he prayed."		1:35	4:42	
He withdrew to the wilderness and prayed.			5:16	
"He went out to the mountain to pray."			6:12	
"Jesus withdrew again to the mountain by himself."				6:15

Continued on following page

Continued from previous page

EVENT	MATTHEW	MARK	LUKE	JOHN
"When he came down from the mountain"	8:1			
"Come away ... to a lonely place."		6:31-32		
"When you pray, go into your room."	6:6			
"Jesus ... withdrew from there in a boat to a lonely place apart."	14:13			
"He went up on the mountain by himself to pray."	14:23			

Subtotal Events & Recordings: 9 Events   10 Times

Jesus Prayed Persistently and Confidently

The unjust judge			18:1-7	
The persistent friend			11:5-13	
"Seek his kingdom, and these things shall be yours as well."	6:31-33		12:29-31	
"Father, I thank thee that thou hast heard me."				11:41-42
"If two of you agree on earth about anything they ask, it will be done for them by my Father in heaven."	18:19			
"Believe that you have received it, and it will be yours."	21:22	11:24		

Subtotal Events & Recordings: 6 Events   8 Times

Jesus Prayed in the Presence of Others

"When all the people were baptized and ... Jesus ... was praying"			3:21	
"As he was praying alone the disciples were with him."			9:18	
"He took with him Peter and John and James, and went up on the mountain to pray"	17:1	9:2	9:28	
"He ordered the crowds to sit ... and taking the five loaves ... looked up to heaven, and blessed."	14:19	6:41	9:15-16	6:10-11

Subtotal Events & Recordings: 4 Events   9 Times

Jesus Prayed Simply

"Do not heap up empty phrases as the Gentiles do."	6:7-8			
Whenever you stand praying, forgive.		11:25		
The Lord's Prayer	6:9-13		11:2-4	
The pharisee and the tax collector			18:9-14	

Subtotal Events & Recordings: 4 Events   5 Times

Total: 23 Events   32 Times

Spread the Word

EVENT	MATTHEW	MARK	LUKE	JOHN
Invite Everyone				
"Come to me **all** who are weary and heavy laden, and I will give you rest."	11:28			
The great banquet	22:1-10		14:15-24	
Share the Mission				
Call of Peter, Andrew, James, and John	4:18-22	1:16-20	5:2-11	
Call of Matthew	9:9	2:14	5:27	
Call of two disciples				1:38-39
Call of Philip				1:43
"In those days came John the Baptist, preaching in the wilderness: 'Repent for the kingdom of heaven is at hand.'"	3:1-2	1:4	3:2-3	
Among those born of women, there has risen no one greater than John the Baptist.	11:11		7:28a	
Choosing the Twelve	10:1-7	3:14-19	6:12-16	
"And he called the twelve together… and he sent them out to preach the kingdom of God and to heal."	(Here the 2 are recorded as 1 event)	6:7a, 12	9:1-2	
After this the Lord appointed seventy others, and sent them on ahead of him… "Whenever you enter a town … say to them, 'The kingdom of God has come near to you.'"			10:8-9	
"For he that is not against us, is for us." ("He who is not with me is against me.")	12:30	9:40	11:23	
"Leave the dead to bury their dead; but as for you, go and proclaim the kingdom of God."	8:22		9:60	
The harvest is plenty, but the laborers are few: Pray therefore the Lord of the harvest to send out laborers into his harvest.	9:37-38		10:2	
But Jesus refused, and said to him, "Go home to your friends, and tell them how much the Lord has done for you …" And he went away and began to proclaim in the Decapolis how much Jesus had done for him; and everyone was amazed.		5:19-20		
Challenge with Love				
"If any want to become my followers, let them deny themselves and take up their cross and follow me."		16:24	8:34	9:23
The Rich Man: "If you would be perfect…come, follow me.	19:16-30	10:17-31	18:18-30	

Total: 18 Events   36 Times

Build Up Treasure in Heaven

EVENT	MATTHEW	MARK	LUKE	JOHN
Detachment				
"Blessed are you poor, for yours is the kingdom of God."	5:3		6:20	
"Sell your possessions, and give alms; provide yourselves with purses that do not grow old, with a treasure in the heavens that does not fail."	6:19-21		12:33-34	
"Therefore do not be anxious.... For the Gentiles seek all these things; and your heavenly Father knows that you need them all."	6:31-33		12:29-31	
"None of you can become my disciple if you do not give up all your possessions."			14:33	
"You cannot serve God and mammon."	6:24		16:13	
"It is easier for a camel to go through the eye of a needle than for someone who is rich to enter the kingdom of God."	19:23-24	10:23, 25	18:24-25	
The rich fool			12:15-21	
The hidden treasure & the pearl of great price	13: 44-45			
Economic Justice				
"You will never get out till you have paid the last penny."	5:25-26		12:57-59	
Taxes to Caesar	22:16-22	12:14-17	20:21-26	
Abundance Mentality				
The widow's offering		12:41-44	21:1-4	
Feeding 5,000 people	14:13-21	6:32-44	9:10-17	6:1-14

Total: 12 Events   25 Times

Seek God's Will

EVENT	MATTHEW	MARK	LUKE	JOHN
Unity with God				
"He who receives me receives him who sent me."	10:40	9:37		
"He who rejects me rejects him who sent me."			10:16	
"No one knows the Father except the Son."	11:27		10:22	
"For as the Father has life in himself, so he has granted the Son also to have life in himself."			5:26	
"I know him, for I come from him."				7:28-29
"If you knew me, you would know my Father also."				8:19
"I do nothing on my own authority but speak thus as the Father taught me."				8:27-29
"If God were your Father, you would love me, for I proceeded and came forth from God."				8:42
"Before Abraham was, I am."				8:58
"I am the good shepherd; I know my own and my own know me, as the Father knows me and I know the Father."				10:14-15
"I and the Father are one."				10:30
"The Father is in me and I am in the Father."				10:38
"He who sees me sees him who sent me."				12:44-45
"The Father who sent me has himself given me commandment what to say and what to speak."				12:49-50

Total: 14 Events   16 Times

Accept Children as Precious

EVENT	MATTHEW	MARK	LUKE	JOHN
Protect Them				
"If any of you put a stumbling-block before one of these little ones ... it would be better ... if... you were drowned in the depth of the sea."	18:6	9:42	17:2	
"See that you do not despise one of these little ones."	18:10			

Continued on following page

Continued from previous page

EVENT	MATTHEW	MARK	LUKE	JOHN
"So it is not the will of my Father who is in heaven that one of these little ones should perish."	18:14			

Welcome Them

EVENT	MATTHEW	MARK	LUKE	JOHN
"Whoever receives one such child in my name receives me."	18:5	9:37	9:48	
"Let the children come to me."	19:13-15	10:13-16	18:15-17	

Be Like Them

EVENT	MATTHEW	MARK	LUKE	JOHN
"Truly, I say to you, unless you change and become like children, you will never enter the kingdom of heaven: Whoever becomes humble like this child is the greatest in the kingdom of heaven."	18:3-4	10:15	18:17	

Total: 6 Events   14 Times

Live with Humility

EVENT	MATTHEW	MARK	LUKE	JOHN
"Blessed are the meek, for they shall inherit the earth."	5:5			
"Many that are first will be last, and the last first."	19:30	10:31		
The laborers in the vineyard	20:1-16			
"And behold, some are last who will be first, and some are first who will be last."			13:30	
"Whoever would be great among you must be your servant, and whoever would be first among you must be your slave."	20:26-28a	10:42-45		
"The greatest among you will be your servant. All who exalt themselves will be humbled, and all who humble themselves will be exalted."	23:11-12			
True greatness		9:33-35	9:46-48	
"For all who exalt themselves will be humbled, and those who humble themselves will be exalted."			14:7-11	
The pharisee and the tax collector			18:9-14	

Total: 9 Events   12 Times

NOTES

The Jesus Priorities: How They Add Up

1. Anthony de Mello, *Awareness* (New York: Image Books, 1990), 129.

2. The average number of events for all the priorities is 17.75; only the top three priorities have more events than the average.

3. Edward Le Joly, *Mother Teresa of Calcutta: A Biography* (San Francisco: Harper and Row, Publishers, 1983), 92.

Priority 1: Heal

1. Thirty-six (36) healings are recorded sixty-three (63) times. The average number of recorded events among the eight priorities is 27. Statistically, the first priority is more than two standard deviations above the average.

Priority 2: Love

1. Matthew 26:6-13 and Mark 14:3-9 are similar; both report that Jesus praises the woman's loving act of humility. In John 12:1-8, the story is assigned to Mary, the sister of Lazarus, not the sinful woman in Luke. Only Luke 7:36-50 records Jesus forgiving the woman, which is consistent with Christ's message of forgiveness and his habit of healing.

2. Quoted in E. W. Trueman Dicken, *The Crucible of Love* (New York: Sheed and Ward, 1963), 41.

Priority 5: Build Up Treasure in Heaven

1. John Kirvan, *Living in the Presence of God: The Everyday Spirituality of Brother Lawrence* (Notre Dame, Ind.: Ave Maria Press, 1997), 31–32.

2. *The Philokalia: The Complete Text*, comp. St. Nikodimos of the Holy Mountain and St. Makarios of Corinth, trans. G. E. H. Palmer, Philip Sherrard, and Kallistos Ware (London: Faber and Faber, 1983), 1:242–43.

3. Thomas à Kempis, *Of the Imitation of Christ,* trans. Justin McCann (New York: New American Library, 1957), 29.

4. *Catherine of Siena: The Dialogue*, trans. Suzanne Noffke (New York: Paulist Press, 1980), 109.

5. Kahlil Gibran, *The Prophet* (New York: Alfred A. Knopf, 1923), 37–38.

6. Jack Kornfield and Christina Feldman, eds., *Soul Food: Stories to Nourish the Spirit and the Heart* (San Francisco: HarperSanFrancisco, 1996), 325.

PRIORITY 6: SEEK GOD'S WILL

1. Fynn, *Mister God, This Is Anna* (New York: Ballantine Books, 2000), 81–82.

PRIORITY 8: PRACTICE HUMILITY

1. C. S. Lewis, *Mere Christianity,* rev. ed. (San Francisco: HarperSanFrancisco, 2001), 125.

2. For the full text see Matt. 20:20-28 and Mark 10:35-45.

MAKING THE JESUS PRIORITIES OUR ESSENTIAL HABITS

1. Encyclopedia Americana International Edition 2006 (Danbury, Conn.: Scholastic Library Publishing, 2006), 647.

2. www.doctorswithoutborders.org/aboutus/

3. Kornfield and Feldman, eds., *Soul Food,* 228.

ABOUT THE AUTHOR

Photo by Keith Burgad

CHRISTOPHER D. MARICLE is a Catholic layman who has been involved in church ministry since his high-school days. He has served as a musician, retreat planner, and Christian summer camp counselor. Professionally, he began working in Catholic schools in 1986 and has served as teacher, elementary school principal, and assistant superintendent of schools. Currently he is a governance consultant for the California School Board Association. He is a graduate of California State University in Sacramento, California, and earned a master's degree in educational leadership from St. Mary's College in Maraga, California.

Christopher lives in California's Sacramento Valley with his wife, Anne, and two children, Sarah and Nicholas.